Ch

M000211108

Chaotic Joy is a delightful conversation about the joy to be found in the midst of motherhood. What I loved best about this book is that it was helpful. Not just inspiring—which it is. Not just thought provoking—which it is. But this book is truly mom-to-mom encouragement that can make a difference for a new mom, or any mom, in the trenches.

Suzanne Eller
Proverbs 31 Ministries Author and Speaker
Author, *The Unburdened Heart* and *The Mended Heart*

At times, motherhood can be daunting and in the midst of it all, it's easy to become weary, worn out, and overwhelmed. In *Chaotic Joy*, Megan Breedlove helps moms embrace the abundant life that Jesus came to give us. With questions at the end of each chapter and Bible study helps in the back, *Chaotic Joy* is a book I definitely recommend—not only for individuals—but for small groups as well.

Stephanie Shott
Founder, The M.O.M. Initiative
Author, *The Making of a Mom*

In *Chaotic Joy*, Megan Breedlove vulnerably and encouragingly mentors fellow moms by sharing personal stories, relatable anecdotes and relevant Scriptures. Mother-to-mother, Megan unveils the secret to abundant joy in mothering—an abundant relationship with Jesus. She reminds us that God is the greatest mother's helper of all-time.

Janet Thompson
Author of 17 books, including *Praying for Your Prodigal Daughter* and *Woman to Woman Mentoring*

Chaotic Joy is a down-to-earth and inspiring book that provides a realistic description of motherhood and the ups and downs that it entails. Megan Breedlove shares simple solutions for strengthening your parenting skills, becoming a more confident woman, and simplifying your walk with God.

Mary Dainty
M.A. Marriage and Family Counseling, LPC-S

With a giant heart, Megan leads us through a hope-filled journey to our high and holy calling of motherhood. In the pages of this book you will discover God is standing right next to you even when the dishes are stacked high and the laundry towers. It's possible to walk in His presence, spend time in prayer, and enjoy the simple and profound gifts of everyday mothering. You will encounter God as He changes your heart and home, and through His love, the chaos of motherhood is transformed into a holy joy.

Lynn Donovan
Author, *Winning Him Without Words* and *Not Alone*

No other author can reach a mother's heart like Meagan Breedlove. *Chaotic Joy* takes the reader on a journey that is not only inspirational, but gives practical steps toward that inner peace we all seek. Great book for individuals, as well as book clubs. Well done!

Judy Gaman,
Co-host of the nationally syndicated radio show *Staying Young*
Co-author, *Age to Perfection: How to Thrive to 100, Happy, Healthy, and Wise.*

Life with kids isn't perfect. And it doesn't have to be. In *Chaotic Joy*, Megan Breedlove encourages and empowers mothers with biblical truths, practical strategies, and inspiring stories that free readers to live fully as a mom and follower of Christ.

Michelle LaRowe
Author, *Working Mom's 411*

Chaotic Joy is a motivating book that inspires the reader to be the best parent they can be, while encouraging gentle patience when one falls short of that ideal. Megan's writing reminds me of my lifelong dream of becoming a mother, which I often forget amid the daily struggles of raising my children. She reminds us that God's love for us is expressed through our love for our children. The practical steps given for bringing prayerful, abundant living into the daily chaos of family life are absolutely indispensable.

Dr. Rochelle McCourtney Gredvig, Psy.D

Finally, a book that captures the beauty and significance of motherhood. Megan's biblical perspective challenges moms to rise above the chaos—and the mundane—to embrace the abundant joy of motherhood. She silences the noise of daily life and focuses on the wisdom of biblical truth, as well as brings heavy doses of encouragement, hope and help. An impressive and outstanding perspective of God's plan for abundant, joy-filled family life!

Susan G. Mathis
Founding Editor, *Thriving Family* magazine
Co-author, *Countdown for Couples: Preparing for the Adventure of Marriage* and *The ReMarriage Adventure: Preparing for a Lifetime of Love & Happiness*

Motherhood is challenging, but it CAN be joyful. That's a message that today's moms don't hear often enough. Megan lovingly takes moms on an honest, transparent journey that acknowledges the difficulties of motherhood, while at the same time equips them with the tools and knowledge they need to take delight in their valuable, God-given role. By internalizing and implementing Megan's hard-won wisdom, moms will discover closer intimacy with Jesus and children that reap immeasurable benefits.

Melinda Means
Co-author, *Mothering from Scratch: Finding the Best Parenting Style for You and Your Family*

Chaotic Joy is the book I needed and longed for as a young mother, but never found. Every word hits the core of your spirit and gives such reassurance and comfort. This is a must read for every mom, no matter how old your children are. Want to know how to rest in the love of God and pass that on to your children? Read this book.

Dineen Miller
Author, *Winning Him Without Words*, *The Soul Saver* and *Not Alone*

Clear the nightstand and put this book within arm's reach. It gives me great pleasure knowing I wasn't the only one who brought my firstborn home and thought, "Now what?" Megan not only shares her mothering mess, but she encourages you to let go of perfection in order to embrace the chaotic joy of motherhood. Whether you've recently been inducted into the motherhood club or have been marching through the trenches for a while, this book is a gem for every mom.

Heather Riggleman
Blogger, Heatherriggleman.com
Author, *Mama Needs a Time Out*

Megan Breedlove again delivers a power-packed truth mothers everywhere should own for themselves. We as mothers would be in a far better place if we viewed our roles and our treasures from this perspective.

Amber Stockton
Award-winning Author

In a magazine era that calls us to "create our best lives," we moms can feel so anxious—so angry—at the day-to-day reality that we give up on creating our best anything. It can be easy to think, as Megan says, that abundant life begins when the kids are grown, or happens in snippets now while (if) they're napping. But it's simply not true. Abundant life isn't the elusive never-quite-ours dream we fear it is. That life is here now, and it's in the companionship of our God, and the messy little mini-me's He's given us to raise. Allow Megan to come alongside you and inspire hope, joy and willingness to jump in to all God has for you today, not only as a mom, but as a woman dearly loved.

Laurie Wallin
Speaker and Certified Life Coach
Author, *Why Your Weirdness Is Wonderful*

chaotic
JOY

Finding **Abundance** in the Messiness of **Motherhood**

Megan Breedlove

Regal

For more information and
special offers from Regal Books, email us at
subscribe@regalbooks.com

Published by Regal
From Gospel Light
Ventura, California, U.S.A.
www.regalbooks.com
Printed in the U.S.A.

All Scripture quotations, unless otherwise indicated, are taken from the
English Standard Version, Copyright © 2001. The *ESV* and *English Standard Version*
are trademarks of Good News Publishers.

Other versions used are
KJV—King James Version. Authorized King James Version.
NIV® Copyright © 1973, 1978, 1984 by Biblica, Inc.™ Used by permission of Zondervan.
All rights reserved worldwide. www.zondervan.com The "NIV" and
"New International Version" are trademarks registered in the United States
Patents and Trademark Office by Biblica, Inc.™
NLT—Scripture quotations marked *NLT* are taken from the *Holy Bible, New Living
Translation,* copyright © 1996, 2004, 2007 by Tyndale House Foundation.
Used by permission of Tyndale House Publishers, Inc., Carol Stream, Illinois 60188.
All rights reserved

© 2014 Megan Breedlove
All rights reserved.

Library of Congress Cataloging-in-Publication Data
Breedlove, Megan.
Chaotic joy : finding abundance in the messiness of motherhood / Megan Breedlove.
pages cm
ISBN 978-0-8307-6971-1 (trade paper)
1. Motherhood—Religious aspects—Christianity. 2. Mothers—Religious life. I. Title.
BV4529.18.B734 2014
248.8'431—dc23
2013040663

Rights for publishing this book outside the U.S.A. or in non-English languages are
administered by Gospel Light Worldwide, an international not-for-profit ministry.
For additional information, please visit www.glww.org, email info@glww.org, or write to
Gospel Light Worldwide, 1957 Eastman Avenue, Ventura, CA 93003, U.S.A.
To order copies of this book and other Regal products in bulk quantities,
please contact us at 1-800-446-7735.

To
The Source of all abundant life.
I look forward to knowing You better
throughout eternity.

Contents

PART 1: RECOGNIZING THE POTENTIAL FOR ABUNDANCE

1. Burden or Blessing? 13
2. Mommy? Mommy?? 22
3. Someone to Talk To 30
4. Sacrifice? Check! 39
5. Say What? 47
6. Knowing God Through Worship 55
7. Shhhhhhh 63
8. Giving 70
9. Frugality 78
10. Fellowship 86

PART 2: ABUNDANT SPIRITUAL BLESSINGS

11. Beyond All We Ask or Imagine 97
12. Abundant Love 104
13. Abundant Peace 111
14. Abundant Joy 122
15. Abundant Strength 130

PART 3: CHANGING YOUR PERSPECTIVE

16. Become Last 143
17. See Your Children as Blessings 150
18. Come Alongside Others 157

PART 4: PRACTICAL ABUNDANCE

19. Abundance in the Mind and Heart 167
20. Abundance in the Home 176
21. Abundance in Relationships 185

A Final Word 199
Bible Study 201
Acknowledgments 217
About the Author 219

Part 1

Recognizing the Potential for Abundance

Burden or Blessing?

It is not until you become a mother that your judgment slowly turns to compassion and understanding.

ERMA BOMBECK

I knew a lot more about parenting before I had children.

When I became pregnant with our first child, my husband and I decided that just before she was born, I would resign my career and begin a new one as a stay-at-home mom. I spent plenty of time dreaming about how my and my baby's life together would go. I planned to spend my days cuddling her and interacting with her. We'd play traditional games such as "How Big Is Baby?" as well as newer, more educational games, with classical music playing in the background. I would dress her in cute, girlie clothing (which would always be clean), and I'd adorn her head with hair bows (which would always stay on). I'd take her on walks or to visit the park.

I definitely would never use television for a babysitter. I wouldn't need to, because we'd be far too busy making arts and crafts or cooking. Discipline? Not a problem. If my child did A, I would do B, and I would get result C. For the more stubborn issues, I might have to repeat B once or twice. We would pray together every day, and we'd have regular family devotions.

Oh, and did I mention that I would be so well organized that I would have time not only to accomplish all this, but also to keep the house clean and prepare delicious, nutritious meals every day?

I had been a successful career woman prior to becoming pregnant. I knew how to work hard, how to organize, and how to prioritize. I could maintain control of chaotic situations with ease, and I could think quickly. Whatever I didn't know about babies, I was sure I could glean from books, the Internet, or my more experienced friends.

I felt completely prepared for motherhood.

My precious baby girl arrived right on schedule, thanks to a planned C-section. I could hardly believe how small and perfect she was. She was the most beautiful baby I had ever seen. Our time together in the hospital was idyllic. I had no idea that motherhood was going to be anything other than the joyous bliss I had envisioned until I realized something: I was going to have to leave the hospital and take my baby home.

When the doctor came to check on me on my last morning there, I told him I wished I didn't have to leave. Naturally, this didn't prevent him from declaring me healthy and ready to be discharged. So my husband and I loaded our bundle of joy into the car, took the obligatory photos, and drove home. We carried Ellie in her infant carrier into the house, and my husband set her down in our brown recliner.

I still remember vividly the question that flashed into my mind: *Now what do we do with her?*

Over the next few days, as complications developed from my surgery and my daughter suffered from feeding issues, any illusions I'd had that motherhood would be nothing but placid contentment were shattered. I realized that motherhood was going to be much more demanding than I had thought. It would be work. *Hard* work.

Even after this realization, I significantly underestimated the amount of work, energy and effort that would be required to do a good job of mothering. True, there are moments in mothering that so overwhelm us with joy that our hearts overflow. But there are also times when the exhaustion is so great that it leaves us feeling like zombies, or when we are so discouraged that we wonder if we're really cut out for this job.

Most of the time, we live somewhere between these two extremes. We put one foot in front of the other, day after day, doing the best we can and hoping it's good enough. The blissful times don't seem to come very frequently, but at least the bad times don't regularly devastate us. It's not as joyous as we had hoped motherhood would be, but everyone we know seems to be in the same boat, so we settle for "making it through."

That's not abundant life.

Two years ago, I attended a major conference on motherhood along with hundreds of other mothers. Though no two of us had the same house or car or children, we all came for the same reason: to receive support and encouragement in our role as moms. I had been looking forward to the conference for months, eager to fellowship with other women and receive affirmation for my role in my children's lives.

The speakers did affirm our value as mothers. They did support and encourage us. But most of them devoted their time to sympathizing with us in the difficulties of motherhood and trying to help us develop strategies to cope with it, rather than focusing on motherhood's positive aspects.

It's true that motherhood is hard. Sometimes, it's *very* hard. It's crazy, chaotic and confusing. But it's also wonderful, joyous and fulfilling. I left the conference grateful that I had some promising new discipline ideas to try, but feeling empty in the part of my heart that longed for someone to say, "Yes, being a mother is work, but it's still the most amazing, breathtaking, fantastic journey we can ever take."

I'll admit that sometimes it doesn't feel fantastic. There are days when I feel more confused than amazed—more beaten down than lifted up. As you probably have as well, I've had days when it seemed that motherhood was more drudgery than delight. But if we buy into Satan's lie that motherhood is nothing more than a calling to change thousands of diapers, do the same housework over and over, and referee countless squabbles about things that don't really matter, we will miss out on the incredible joy that God has planned for us.

You see, a calling to motherhood is much more than a calling to the myriad tasks associated with it. A calling to motherhood is a calling to abundant life.

Can Motherhood Really Be Abundant?

Many things in motherhood are abundant. Diapers that need changing? Check. Meals to prepare? Check. Housework to do—and do again? Check. Clothes to buy and forms to fill out and playdates to schedule? Check. But motherhood itself? Can motherhood itself be abundant?

Jesus gives us the answer to that question. After explaining to the Pharisees that He is the Good Shepherd—the One who tenderly loves and cares for His sheep—He tells them:

> The thief comes only to steal and kill and destroy. I came that they may have life and have it abundantly (John 10:10).

Jesus' intent was to explain how He related to His sheep—in other words, to those who follow Him. When He calls us, it is not to destruction. It is to abundant life.

If that's true (and because Jesus said it, we know that it is), He came so that you and I could have abundant life—not a miserable, beaten-down existence, but glorious, magnificent life! Not just in heaven one day, but here, now, on earth. And if *that's* true, then motherhood *is* abundant life. We don't have to wait until our children are grown and we're empty-nesters to discover abundant life. We don't have to hope for a time when things settle down enough for us to experience abundant life—because we can experience it here and now, in the midst of the chaos. Motherhood *is* the abundant life God promised us.

So why doesn't it feel abundant?

Roadblocks to Abundance

There are four major roadblocks to experiencing motherhood as rich and rewarding. You may have experienced one or all of these to some degree.

The first obstacle is thinking that we can only experience abundant life when all our circumstances are to our liking. In other words, if the house is tidy, the children are clean and well-behaved, and I can afford a babysitter frequently enough to go out and do things on my own, *then* I can be content. Otherwise, forget it.

Moms, if this is your attitude, you are doomed to disappointment. *A lot* of disappointment. Rarely will everything go perfectly at the same time. If you can only be satisfied when life is what you would consider perfect, well, you won't be satisfied very often.

Fortunately, God has made it possible for us to enjoy abundant life even when circumstances are very different from what we would wish—when things are unpleasant, confusing, or just plain chaotic. That's what this book is about. We can have abundant life in the midst of circumstances we would change if we could. But before we talk about how that happens, let's look at three other potential roadblocks to experiencing abundant life right now.

The second roadblock is longing excessively for what we used to have. Before becoming a mother, I had a career I loved. I enjoyed the work. I liked and appreciated the people with whom I worked. My job was fun. It was exciting. It was never the same two days in a row.

When my baby girl was born, I went from being a high-energy person in a fast-paced career to a perpetually tired person in a career that was so slow-paced that it seemed like my grass grew at breakneck speed in comparison. It felt like going from 60 to 0 instantly. I was bored, lonely and grieving.

I loved my daughter with all my heart, but I missed my job, my coworkers, and my being a part of the workplace. Skills I had worked so hard to attain no longer mattered, because they weren't relevant to my new position. Worst of all, I felt isolated.

My husband was wonderful to be with when he was home, but he had a full-time job. Many of my friends were at work—some at the very workplace I had left. My other friends all had families of their own and wanted to spend time with them in the evenings, which was when my husband was gone. Even the adrenaline rushes of my work were gone. In their place were hormones and the baby blues.

I finally had what I had always wanted—a precious child—but I grieved for what I could no longer have.

The ancient Israelites would have empathized with me. They were oppressed by the Egyptians for 400 years. As if that weren't enough, God allowed their suffering to increased temporarily before He finally delivered them from slavery. Then He showed Himself mighty, performing plague after plague, until at last Pharaoh begged the Israelites to leave. *Great!* they must have thought. *We're out of here!* But not so fast. Pharaoh changed his mind, and he and his army caught up to the fleeing slaves. Fortunately, that was no problem for God. He parted the Red Sea, allowed the Israelites to cross through, and then caused the waters to flow back into place and drown the Egyptians.

When the Israelites became thirsty on their journey and complained about it, God provided water from a rock. When they got hungry, they once again began to complain:

> If only we had died by the LORD's hand in Egypt! There we sat around pots of meat and ate all the food we wanted, but you have brought us out into this desert to starve this entire assembly to death (Exod. 16:3, *NIV*).

Incredibly, despite their former suffering, they were longing for what they'd had before!

For me, even though I had loved my job, being home with my precious daughter was infinitely preferable to being at work. But despite knowing I'd made the right choice for our family, the longing I felt for what had gone before still interfered with my ability to delight in my current circumstances.

What do you long for that you used to have, but no longer do? Free time? The carefree days of singleness or childlessness? Spending money? It's not wrong to miss those things. We should enjoy the blessings God gives us, and the natural counterpart to that is missing them when they're gone. But we must learn to wholeheartedly embrace our present (and future) that doesn't include those things, knowing that God has planned something even better for us.

The third roadblock to experiencing motherhood as abundant is being unable to see past the unpleasant details of our calling. If we raise our gazes no higher than the mound of dishes in the sink or the piles of laundry on the floor, we won't be looking nearly high enough. Putting too much emphasis on the details usually causes us to narrow our focus to ourselves. Many times, the thought process goes something like this: *Just look at all these things I have to take care of. I'll never get caught up. Seems like I'm the only one who cares about getting things done around here.*

That kind of self-centered focus rarely leads to inner peace and an appreciation of our status as mothers. Instead, it causes us to resent those who are most dear to us and to spend our time bogged down in self-pity instead of lifted up in joy.

It was never God's intention for our primary focus to be on the nuts and bolts of our day-to-day existence. Granted, as mothers, there are many things we have to take care of. We are responsible for the care and nurturing of our children and the orderly management of our homes. But when these things become our primary focus, that's sin.

Pursuing the calling God has given us should never detract from our relationship with Him. Yet too often, we set our sights on the earthly details of life and forget to gaze adoringly at the Author of Life. We spend more time bemoaning the fact that the living room is a mess *again* than we do contemplating God's majesty.

I know it's easy to get bogged down in the logistics of living. I have five young children. Believe me, I understand. But if you or I allow *anything*, even our children, to make us forget to focus on God, that's idolatry. And idolatry will never lead to spiritually abundant living.

Making a Godward focus our first priority, however, and relegating the details of our lives to secondary status renders unto God His due and puts other things in their proper places. When we have our lives ordered according to God's design, we will begin to experience abundant motherhood.

The fourth roadblock applies not just to mothers, but to every person God has ever created. It is failing to realize that abundant life is to be experienced not through circumstances that make us happy, but through a relationship with God.

Too often, we look to motherhood (or some other aspect of our lives) to meet needs that can only be fulfilled by God Himself. Motherhood will not provide enough of a sense of significance to fill the empty place in our heart that longs to know we are worthwhile. Being a mother might introduce us to fascinating people, but it won't ultimately be the companion to our souls that we long for. In the end, motherhood is a marvelous blessing, but it was never meant to carry the burden of having to meet needs that only God can truly fulfill—a burden we too often assign to it.

When we look to the role or circumstances of motherhood to provide for all of our emotional needs, we are guaranteed to be disappointed. God has given us certain needs, and He has ordained that in this world, some of those needs will never be completely fulfilled apart from Him. Instead of trying to manufacture fulfillment and contentment for ourselves through our circumstances, we must look to God Himself for our deepest satisfaction.

In calling us to be mothers, God grants us two priceless gifts. The first is the privilege of being a mom and of knowing and loving our precious children. The second is the privilege of coming to know Him more intimately. The first gift can never fulfill our deepest longings; the second gift is the only thing that can.

You see, our spirits were made to desire God and to need Him completely and desperately. Through motherhood, God calls us to a lifestyle that can result in knowing Him in ways in which we would never have come to know Him otherwise. *That*, my friend, is abundant life!

Getting Started

So yes, motherhood can be abundant, because it provides abundant opportunities to know God. That's what this book is about: ways that each mom, no matter her circumstances, can experience more abundant life. We'll start with one specific way God has chosen for us to get to know Him that we wouldn't have been able to experience if we weren't mothers.

Abundant Living Action Steps

1. List the things about motherhood that came as a surprise to you. Were any of these upsetting to you?
2. Which roadblock to abundance are you most prone to experience? Are you experiencing it now? What can you do about this issue so that it no longer blocks you from experiencing the abundant life that God promises? How would you like God to help? Ask Him to help you in that way.
3. What would abundant motherhood look like to you? Do you think this is a realistic picture of motherhood? Discuss this with God, and ask Him whether or not you're being realistic.

For a more in-depth study of the topics of each chapter, see the Bible study at the end of this book.

2

Mommy? Mommy??

My mother's love has always been a sustaining force for our family.
MICHELLE OBAMA

Have you ever thought of changing your name to something other than Mommy?

I have. I remember one day in particular; it had been one of "those" days. I was tired of hearing my "name" over and over, usually followed by some request I considered either annoying or unimportant (or both). So when my daughter called for me for the umpteenth time, I didn't answer right away.

"Mommy?" she called out.

I didn't say anything. I wanted at least to finish putting the last few folded clothes back in dresser drawers before I had to turn my attention to something else.

"Mommy? Mommy??"

I heard little footsteps coming closer, and then Lindsey appeared in the bedroom doorway. "Oh, there you are, Mommy," she said.

"My name's not Mommy," I responded.

Lindsey looked understandably confused. Then, "Yes it is," she said. "Mommy?"

I couldn't fool Lindsey. Confuse her for a moment, yes, but not fool her. She knew good and well that I was her mother and she was my daughter. She understood the parent-child relationship.

You and I once understood the parent-child relationship from the perspective of a child too. But when we became parents, we began to understand it from a different perspective than we ever had before.

A New Perspective on the Parent-Child Relationship

We began to learn what it's like to love a child, which is a love that is different from every other. It's a love that's all-consuming. This kind of love requires self-sacrifice on the loved one's behalf, even to the extent of offering up our physical life if that's what it takes. We're willing to accept this responsibility, and we do our best to be the kind of loving parent we've always imagined ourselves being. A parent who loves her children far more than she loves herself. A parent who is willing to put her child first, even when it's unpleasant. A parent who will love her child *no matter what*.

Becoming a parent is an incredible lesson in love that is virtually impossible to learn any other way. As we grow as parents, we grow in our love for our children, learning to love them more and more deeply each day.

But we don't always apply our knowledge of our earthly parent-child relationships to the relationship we have with God.

Over and over, Scripture describes God as our Father in heaven. Check out just a few verses:

To all in Rome who are loved by God and called to be saints: Grace and peace to you from God our Father and from the Lord Jesus Christ (Rom. 1:7, *NIV*).

To our God and Father be glory for ever and ever. Amen (Phil. 4:20, *NIV*).

May he strengthen your hearts so that you will be blameless and holy in the presence of our God and Father when our Lord Jesus comes with all his holy ones (1 Thess. 3:13, *NIV*).

May our Lord Jesus Christ himself and God our Father, who loved us and by his grace gave us eternal encouragement and good hope, encourage your hearts and strengthen you in every good deed and word (2 Thess. 2:16-17, *NIV*).

Jesus referred to God the same way many times:

For this reason the Jews tried all the harder to kill him; not only was he breaking the Sabbath, but he was even calling God his own Father, making himself equal with God (John 5:18, *NIV*).

No one has seen the Father except the one who is from God; only he has seen the Father (John 6:46, *NIV*).

Jesus said, "Do not hold on to me, for I have not yet returned to the Father. Go instead to my brothers and tell them, 'I am returning to my Father and your Father, to my God and your God'" (John 20:17, *NIV*).

We know that the Bible calls God our Father, but we don't often stop to think about what this means. If we do think about it, we may conclude that God's being our Father means that He's in charge and gets to tell us what to do. But the Bible says, in 1 John 3:1, that God's being our Father is all about love: "How great is the love the Father has lavished on us, that we should be called children of God! And that is what we are!" (*NIV*).

It's amazing. It's incredible. It's beyond belief that God would call us His children. Oh, we'd understand if He wanted to call us His slaves. Even that is far more than we deserve. But to call us His beloved children? Mind-blowing.

Granted, God is indeed absolutely in charge, and He does have the right to tell us to do anything He wants us to do. But His Fatherhood means so much more than that. It means all the tender things we long for from a parent, whether we ever received those things from our earthly parents or not. It means all the loving, compassionate things we do for our own children, times a billion, because God is perfectly loving and we are not.

The apostle Matthew writes, "If you then, who are evil, know how to give good gifts to your children, how much more will your Father who is in heaven give good things to those who ask him!" (Matt. 7:11, *NIV*). So if we can give the gift of loving parenting to our own children, how much greater a gift of *perfectly* loving parenting can God give to us?

Being perfectly loved sure sounds like abundant life to me!

Yet amazingly, there's more. Let's look at four things we learn through parenting our own children and then consider how these lessons factor into the abundant life Jesus has promised us.

What We Learn Through Parenting

One of the first things we learn is that our love for our children is based on their identity as our children, not on anything they do or fail to do. By the time that child is placed in our arms, whether she came to us through birth or adoption, we have already begun to love her. Why? Because she's done something for us? No. In fact, if your child comes into your life as an infant, she requires a lot from you without giving much back. You don't love her because she's done something. You love her because she's yours.

I remember sitting in the hospital with my firstborn shortly after her birth. For the moment, the room was empty, and we were alone. Suddenly, into my mind flashed this thought: *What if the next person through that door is not a nurse to help us, but someone who wants to harm us?* The thought that someone would try to harm my precious child chilled my blood. I knew in that instant that I would do anything it took to keep my baby safe. Anything. Because she was *my daughter*.

Likewise, God's love for us is based on our identity as His children, not on anything we have done. There was never anything we could do to earn or merit His love. In fact, there have been many things we did or failed to do that would seem to preclude His ever loving us at all. How could a holy God love people who are as sinful as we are? Yet He chose to do just that. He chose to extend His love to us as His cherished children. We get to enjoy His completely, perfectly wonderful love for us simply because we're His.

I can't imagine much that would make life feel more abundant than knowing that we are deeply, completely, perfectly loved. Nothing we have done or ever will do can change that, because God's love for us is based on our identity, not our actions. You and I can go through life knowing that we are loved—not just with the same all-encompassing love with which we love our own children, but with a love that's a billion times greater.

Completely, perfectly loved. What could be better than that? But wait; there's more!

As parents, we also love our children with a permanent love. Yes, they drive us crazy sometimes, but we never stop loving them. True, there are days when we don't love their actions very much, but we always love *them*. Nothing our children could do will ever cause us to stop loving them. Their behavior could grieve us, yes, but it can't extinguish our love.

In the same way, God loves us forever, no matter what we've done in the past or will do in the future. Remember how we said His love for us is based not upon our actions but upon our identity? That's another way we know it's permanent. Our identity will never change. We will always be His children. God has chosen us to be part of His family, and He's not going to "un-choose" us. Nor is He going to allow us to remain in His family but only permit us to sleep on the patio and eat leftovers, never joining the rest of the family at the table. He does now, and will always, treat us as *beloved*, not as merely tolerated. We are beloved daughters of God, and we always will be.

"God is not man, that he should lie, or a son of man, that he should change his mind" (Num. 23:19). That means that He will never change His mind about loving us. So not only are we completely, perfectly loved, but we're also loved that way forever! What could be more abundant than that?

Think about how you feel on Christmas, when your child is just about to open *the* gift—the one he or she has been begging for—which you purchased, wrapped and placed under the tree. Think about the anticipation you feel as your child tears into the wrapping paper, and then . . . the delight! Oh, the rapture on your child's face and the excitement in your own heart. You love to give good gifts to your children.

God loves to give good gifts to us too. Somehow, many of us have gotten this idea that God provides for us because He has to. That He only does it out of duty. But we're oh-so-wrong!

Remember how we said God is crazy about us, and will be forever? He loves to shower us with His blessings. In fact, He invites us to test Him and see if He won't open heaven's storehouses and pour out His blessings upon us (see Mal. 3:10). That hardly sounds like someone who doesn't enjoy giving.

That delight you have when you get to give your child something he or she wants? God has a far greater delight when He gets to give good things to you.

Not only do you have a Father who will love you madly and passionately forever, and who delights to give you things because He's crazy about you, but you also have a Father who cares what happens to you.

A few months ago, we were hosting a play date at our house that wasn't going well. The other mom's children weren't obeying their mom or me, and they were making a huge mess. Matters got worse when Kenny came to me, tears in his eyes, and told me the other boy had said something mean to him. "What did he say?" I asked.

"He said I was stupid," Kenny said, his lower lip trembling as he tried not to cry.

At that point, I was ready to jump into the situation and straighten it out. Nobody gets to call my son "stupid" without hearing about it from me. I cared deeply about what had been said to Kenny. (Fortunately, the boy's mother corrected him, so I didn't have to.)

If I cared that much about a comment that was relatively minor in the grand scheme of life, how much more does God care when bad or even tragic things happen to us? Oh, He cares deeply.

Never think that just because He doesn't prevent something painful from happening, He doesn't care. Far from it. God has His reasons for causing or allowing something, but make no mistake about it: He always cares, and He always suffers when we suffer. John 11:35 tells us that Jesus cried when His friend Lazarus died and He saw how deeply Lazarus's friends and relatives were grieving. The passage goes on to tell us that even in Jesus' day, the intensity of His grief was noted as remarkable. Jesus was deeply moved by what had happened to His friend as well as to those left behind, and He is deeply moved today when we face tragic circumstances, because He is the same yesterday, today and forever (see Heb. 13:8).

You and I can better understand our Father because we're parents too. We do some of the same things He does: train up our children, administer consequences, give rewards, offer comfort, have fun with our children, and provide for our children. We can't completely understand God because we're not divine, but we can get a glimpse of what He thinks and feels by watching Him at His parenting. We can also multiply our good and righteous feelings toward our children by a factor of "infinity," and we begin to get an idea of how our Father feels about us. He loves us like crazy, loves us forever, delights in giving good things to us, and cares about what happens to us.

Those are some of the things I want my children to be able to say about me: that I loved them with all my heart and without ceasing, that I loved giving them things, and that I cared deeply about what happened to them. When they go out into the world, I want them to have the confidence that comes from knowing that all these things are true. And if they can have a soul-building confidence because of love that comes from a mere earthly parent, how much more abundant life and confidence can you and I have because God does all these things perfectly?

One reason God made us moms is so that we can understand Him better as we try to imitate Him in our parenting relationships. We get to know Him by taking the ways we feel and think about our own children and considering them in the light of how He feels about us. So the next time you find yourself bursting with love or compassion for your child, or delighting in giving your child something, remind yourself that God feels the same way about you—only more so. Get to know Him as your Father—and gain the foundation for the abundant life He has promised.

Abundant Living Action Steps

1. If God is your perfect Father, what is He like? Write it down, and then spend a few minutes in prayer, praising and thanking Him for how amazing a Parent He is.
2. Is there anything you need God to give you right now? Remember that He delights to give. Ask Him directly for what you need.

For a more in-depth study of the topics of each chapter, see the Bible study at the end of this book.

3

Someone to Talk To

*You, O Lord, have called us to watch and pray. Therefore, whatever may
be the sin against which we pray, make us careful to watch against it,
and so have reason to expect that our prayers will be answered.
In order to perform this duty aright, grant us grace to preserve a sober,
equal temper, and sincerity to pray for your assistance. Amen.*
SUSANNA WESLEY

Before I had children, I had plenty of time for prayer, meditation
and study. I would get off work at 11 P.M., come home, and spend
the next hour with God. I'd pray, read my Bible, and work through
a study I was doing. Sometimes, I would sing or listen to worship
music. Those were spiritually beautiful times as I sat or kneeled
before the Lord and learned to know and love Him more.

When my first daughter, Ellie, was born, I recognized that, more
than ever, I needed a close relationship with God. Naturally, since
my pre-baby routine had resulted in much meaningful time spent
with the Lord, I attempted to recreate it. The only problem was
that with a newborn, finding an uninterrupted hour was next to
impossible. But because I was determined to maintain a growing
relationship with God, I tried every way I could think of to make
my quiet time happen as I thought it should.

I tried to "seize the moment" whenever Ellie was sleeping and
have my quiet time then, only to find that, many times, I was too
exhausted to concentrate. I tried to let the housework go and have
my devotions instead, with the result that the housework got let go,
all right, but my quiet times still didn't always happen. I thought

3

about getting up earlier, but I was desperate for sleep. I attempted to stay up later, but found that sometimes my eyes would start to close while I was reading. I did find a short devotional magazine from which I could read the day's entry before going to bed, but doing that didn't seem like enough. And prayer time? Closing my eyes to pray early in the morning or late at night was an invitation to fall asleep.

I wish I could say that within a couple months, I figured out when and how to work a satisfying quiet time into my routine, but I can't. When I had another child and my time became even less my own, I became more and more frustrated at my inability to do what I thought I should be doing in the area of devotions.

I tried to find times when I could leave my husband in charge of the kids and get off by myself for some meaningful time with God. I was able to do that occasionally, but not every day. I tried taking advantage of available moments during the day, only to be interrupted by little voices calling for me. I tried everything I could think of. I tried harder, even when I wasn't sure what "trying harder" should look like. I was certain that if I could just figure out how to do it, I could make a meaningful quiet time happen.

Sometime before the birth of my third child, Lindsey, I established a Bible reading and Scripture memory plan. I began a program of reading through the Bible in a year and memorizing two verses a week. Finally, my regular quiet time was happening. This plan worked for a while, even after Lindsey was born.

Somewhere along the way, though, the plan stopped working for me. It was still a good plan, but it didn't seem to be fitting my spiritual needs anymore. Something was missing; I just wasn't sure what. So now what was I going to do? I still remember the frustration I felt at thinking that my last-ditch effort had failed. *Why is this so hard?* I asked myself repeatedly. *Why can't I make this work?*

It was at that point, when I was completely and totally frustrated with trying to make a quiet time happen properly, that I became most teachable. You see, up until then, I'd had my own idea of what a quiet time should look like, and I was trying my hardest to make it happen the way I thought it should. But when I reached the point of having to admit my complete inability to manufacture a meaningful quiet time, or even make the space in my schedule for one, I began to learn what God desired for me in the area of spending time with Him.

Yes, He wanted me to spend time with Him every day. God knows that in order for me to be close to Him, I must spend time with Him. I was right about that. But I was completely wrong to assume that my post-baby quiet times should always look like my pre-baby quiet times, because that was never God's intention.

Sometimes, I do still manage to get some uninterrupted time for study, and I relish those times of spiritual refreshment. But for the most part, my time with God looks different now. That's okay. God knew what my life would look like once I became a mother. He is well aware of the time it takes to nurture my precious children. After all, He is the one who gave those children to me, and He was not unaware of the time commitment when He did so. He doesn't necessarily expect your quiet times to continue in the same way they did before, either. If He still gives you an uninterrupted hour for time with Him every day, that's great. Take advantage of it. But for most of us, assuming that we will have that every day is unrealistic. After all, everything else changes when we have a baby. Why would we think our relationship with God won't change too?

God hasn't given most of us daily, large blocks of time for anything personal. But He *has* given us all the time we need to maintain a vitally intimate relationship with Him. How can I say that, when there are some days when it's hard to get a shower before 3:00 (or ever!) because I'm so busy? Because I know what God intends for us.

God's Ultimate Desire for Us

What is God's deepest desire for you? That you be a great wife? That you be a patient, loving mother? That you minister to others around you?

These are all good things, and they will probably be byproducts of what God most wants for you, but they are not His ultimate goal. God's ultimate goal is that you (and I) be conformed to the image of His Son, Jesus. Because He knows that a relationship with Him is necessary in order for you to become more like Jesus, God will never call you to anything in life that must, of necessity, detract from that relationship.

How can we reconcile this idea with the fact that little feet pitter-patter toward the door any time they sense that we are alone, or not-so-little voices start screaming in the living room the minute we sit down in the bedroom to have our devotions? How can we say that the calling of motherhood doesn't detract from our relationship with God?

For one thing, just because the kind of time we spend with Him once we become moms looks different and is structured differently doesn't mean that it's any "less" than it was before. True, we may have to develop a whole different routine from what we're used to—or, better yet, the flexibility to deal with the lack of a stable routine in our devotions. But that's okay! In fact, it's great! Because that's some of what God wants us to learn.

He wants us to learn a whole new way of relating to Him. He wants to permeate our lives—to *be* our lives—not just be confined to a specified activity or a certain amount of time during the day.

All Day with Him

I read a quotation once that went something like this: "It took not having an hour with Him to realize that I had all day with Him." I wish I had been the one to write that. Or, more accurately, I wish I had possessed the wisdom contained in those words much earlier in my life.

As a new mom, I was too caught up in wanting to do everything "right" to see that there might be another way to do things. As a slightly more experienced mom, beginning to deal with issues of correction and discipline of my children, I knew that it was imperative that I stay close to God—not only for my sake, but also for my children's—and I tried even harder to make things work the one "right" way. As a mom of three young children, I knew that my children were watching my example, and I was determined that I would provide a godly one.

What I didn't realize was that being a godly mom would look different from being a godly single woman or wife, down to the very details of my quiet times.

Perhaps the biggest difference in my walk with God was realizing that my time with Him would now last all day instead of being confined to a single hour. As a mom, spending time in communion with God was no longer something I could do at my convenience and in my preferred location. Now, my devotions would have to take place throughout both the day and the house.

Pray Without Ceasing

I had heard of Brother Lawrence, the seventeenth-century monk who wrote the letters that became the basis for the book *Practicing the Presence of God*. In one of his letters, Brother Lawrence described how he almost felt that the bells that called the monks to prayer were an interruption of his time with God.

That's what I need, I thought to myself. *How do I get that?*

The answer is simple. It's not easy, but it's simple. I had to learn to pray in a different way. Without the possibility of relegating my quiet time to one specific hour in one specific chair, I knew I must learn to pray continuously if I wanted to continue to have any kind of meaningful prayer life.

So how does a mom who doesn't have an hour—or even 10 minutes—of uninterrupted time to pray find multiple times throughout the day? First, she redefines what constitutes acceptable prayer.

Somehow, we Christians often get it into our heads that the only acceptable way to pray is to sit quietly (or perhaps kneel) with our heads bowed and eyes closed. This is far from the truth. There are many examples in Scripture of Jesus praying with other postures. The Gospels describe Jesus looking up toward heaven as He prayed, praying as He walked, and praying loudly so that a crowd could hear Him.

We know that all of Jesus' prayers were acceptable to the Father, so we can conclude from these passages that there is not only one right posture for praying.

What does this mean for us? It means that we can pray as we stand washing dishes. *Lord, thank You that we have enough food. Thank You for all of the people gathered around our table.* Maybe as we wash our daughter's special cup or our son's favorite plate, we pray, *Thank You for this precious child, and for the money to buy extra things like Hello Kitty plates.* Maybe we pray for family members who were absent for that meal.

We can even pray as we do laundry. *Lord, thank You for providing our clothing. Thank You that I don't have to go down to a stream somewhere to wash it. Thank You for detergent I don't have to make myself and for the blessing of an electric dryer.*

As we load the family into the car for a trip, perhaps we pray for safety on the journey. As I sit here, listening to the rain hitting the roof of my house as I write, my heart is moved to offer thanks to God for the shelter over my head. We can pray any time, anywhere, with all different kinds of requests (see Eph. 6:18). God uses motherhood to teach us to live in constant, varied communion with Him rather than restricting our time together to a specific hour or location.

Seize the Moment

We can pray anytime, anywhere. But what about reading our Bible or other devotional materials? It's much harder (and more dangerous) to read while driving a car than it is to pray while doing so. How do we get time enough to sit down and concentrate on even a brief passage of Scripture?

First, we have to learn to seize the moment. Most of our households don't adhere strictly enough to a schedule that we can count on reading our Bibles at the same time every day. If we want to read God's Word, we have to find time where it might not look like there is any.

Some of the things that didn't work for me might work for you. It may fit well with the rhythms of your household for you to rise early or stay up late. But if you're like me, and you know that trying to plan on a specific time each day is doomed to failure and will discourage you, you will have to learn to seize the moment.

When you put the baby down to sleep, take a few minutes and read your Bible. I know there's housework waiting for you, but sometimes the better thing to do is to tend to your spiritual needs and let the dishes soak a bit. While you wait for the kids to finish soccer practice, you can sit in the stands or in the car and read your Bible. Many Christian bookstores have pretty holders for Scripture verse cards. You can put one on your kitchen windowsill and look at it every time you come to the sink.

Another way to seize time is to redeem it from other pursuits. There are many things you have to do as a mom that can't be pushed aside, at least not for long. But are there any unnecessary activities that steal your time?

For me, a big temptation is to spend too much time on the computer. I enjoy playing games, managing my Facebook account, and doing other things. If I'm not careful, I can spend way too much time online. Granted, I have fun, but it also means that I have less time for other pursuits. Each of us has the same 24 hours in a day. If you spend too much time doing things that will burn up like chaff, you're not going to have as much time for things that count for eternity.

Maybe, if you truly desire to have the time you need with the Lord, it will mean you no longer have time for your book club or even some of your church activities. Maybe you'll have to give up something else that seems like a priority right now. Oh, precious mommy, don't hesitate! If there's anything coming between you and God, throw it aside. Count it all loss for the surpassing joy of knowing Christ Jesus, your Lord (see Phil. 3:7-8). As Jim Elliot said, "He is no fool who gives what he cannot keep to gain what he cannot lose."

Freedom from the Law

Once you realize that your relationship with the Lord doesn't have to fit within certain parameters of time and location, you will begin to discover a glorious freedom.

The bondage often starts when we're growing up. As we mature in the faith, well-meaning people teach us various strategies for a quiet time. There's nothing wrong with their doing this; in fact, I do it with my own children. The bondage begins when we somehow get the idea that quiet time has to be done a certain way in order to be done right.

The Pharisees were experts at this kind of thinking. They had determined the right way to do everything. If you did things their way, you were holy. If you didn't, you were a sinner. Did Jesus praise them for their rigidity? Quite the opposite! In fact, He called them whitewashed tombs—pretty on the outside but dead on the inside (see Matt. 23:27). He also chastised them for laying burdens of obedience on people that were too heavy for them to bear (see Matt. 23:4).

Jesus knew that a relationship with God comes not through keeping a set of stringent requirements or doing things a certain way, but through being in loving relationship with Him. In fact, when asked what the greatest commandment was, Jesus responded, "Love the Lord your God with all your heart and with all your soul and with all your strength and with all your mind" (Luke 10:27). He came not to impose more requirements on us, but to make things simpler for us. All we have to do, He said (though it's huge), is to love God with everything we are. He didn't say we had to love God exactly like our neighbor loves Him.

There is marvelous freedom in how you relate to God. You are different from every other person God ever has made or ever will make, so your relationship with Him will be different from any other. How you spend your time with Him may be different from how your best friend does her devotions, and that's okay. There is freedom in that, dear friend!

You may find it helpful to have a plan for what you want to do during your quiet time so that you can get the most benefit out of it. But if you can't follow your plan, don't despair. God has something better in mind. Remember, He will never call you to something that will make your relationship with Him suffer.

Instead, He has called you to the glorious abundance of remaining in His presence anywhere, all day long.

Abundant Living Action Steps

1. What would you like your quiet time to look like? Discuss it with God. Ask Him what He wants it to look like.
2. If you haven't had your quiet time today, why not have it now? If you can't have it now, can you make a plan for doing it later today?

For a more in-depth study of the topics of each chapter, see the Bible study at the end of this book.

Sacrifice? Check!

*The interesting thing about being a mother is that
everyone wants pets, but no one but me cleans the kitty litter.*
MERYL STREEP

I mentioned earlier that I knew motherhood would entail quite
a bit of sacrifice. But I never realized how many of the sacrifices
would involve giving a child the food from my plate instead of
asking him or her to eat the food on his or her own plate. My kids
have each gone through a mooching stage (Timmy is still in it),
where whatever's on my plate looks vastly more delicious than the
same food on the child's own plate. Or where whatever snack I
have just fixed for myself looks so yummy that to have it *right now*.

I also never realized how much privacy I would lose. I remember when I was in the hospital after giving birth to Timmy, our
fifth child. My husband had brought the other kids to the hospital
so they could spend some time with me and especially with their
new little brother. While my husband was there, I decided to seize
the opportunity to take a shower.

I made it all the way into the shower by myself. I turned the
warm water on and stood there, soaking it up and allowing it to
relax my body. I remember that it felt so good.

I almost didn't hear the door to the bathroom open.

Figuring someone needed to use the toilet, I continued my
shower. That is, until I heard, "Mommy? Can we come in there?"
and saw Lindsey's and Jessica's little faces peeking around the edge
of the shower curtain.

Giving a child some of our own food or even sharing the shower is hardly the biggest sacrifice we're called to make as moms,
however (though depending on the food, that might rank right
up there). We're called upon daily to sacrifice all kinds of things,
whether we want to or not, *when* we want to or not. For example,
see how many of the following you have had to sacrifice recently:

- Food (or at least hot food)
- Sleep
- Time
- Money
- Sleep
- Your preferences
- Your plans
- Sleep
- Energy
- Prayer/devotional time
- Sleep
- Education/career
- Sanity
- Adult conversation
- Sleep
- Peace of mind
- Personal space
- Privacy
- Sleep
- Time alone
- New clothes
- Haircuts
- Sleep
- Favorite TV shows
- Clean house/car
- Your rights
- Sleep

- Your toothpaste
- Your waistline
- Going through museums or grocery stores at a reasonable speed
- Sleep

You can probably think of many other things that aren't on this list that you've been called to sacrifice. Some of them are easier to give up than others (can you tell which one is hard for me?), but all require the denial of self so that your children can have what they need.

We know going into this thing called motherhood that we're going to have to sacrifice. But most of us probably figure that this sacrifice will come mainly in the areas of buying diapers and losing a little sleep now and then. We don't realize the hundreds of big and small ways we'll be called upon to sacrifice that aren't found in any of the parenting books.

Sacrifice is never completely easy; it requires you to relinquish something that has value to you. When the sacrificial moment comes, you may be tempted to hold onto your possessions or your rights with all your might instead of giving them up for your children's sake.

I'm more willing to sacrifice some times than others. You probably are too. On some days, when our children come to us with a request, it's relatively easy to put our plans aside and say, "Sure, I'll play with you." On other days, we'd rather do just about anything than have to play baby dolls one more time, and it's hard to say, "Sure! I'd love to." If we say it at all, we say it through gritted teeth.

At those times when we know we should say yes, we have a choice: We can say no, thereby removing our need to sacrifice; we can say yes, but grudgingly; or we can say yes joyfully.

Joyfully? Are you kidding? I already played that game three million times. I don't have it in me to do one more!

But what if I told you that sacrifice can help you know God better? What if I told you that sacrifice can connect you with the heart of God in a very real and powerful way? Think you might be interested?

The Jews of Jesus' day had a custom called fasting. Fasting usually involved abstaining from food and was done on a regular basis so that the person fasting could devote him- or herself to prayer. Fasting could be either personal or corporate. Sometimes, if the people were facing a particularly thorny problem, they would fast and pray corporately until God granted the solution to their problem. Back then, it was assumed that all devout people fasted. Of course, sometimes people fasted for the purpose of making a point about how holy they were, but that didn't cause Jesus to condemn fasts. Instead, He simply gave instructions on how fasts were to be done.

In Matthew 6:16, Jesus was telling the people how to fast, and He exhorted them not to look miserable while doing it. Apparently, some of the Pharisees had made it a point to "disfigure" their faces (yikes! I can only imagine what that means) so as to look particularly gloomy when fasting. That way, people would know they were fasting and would be impressed with how holy they were.

This was contrary to Jesus' instructions, however—which, by the way, He began by saying, "*When* you fast" (emphasis added). Not *if* you fast, but *when*. He communicated the expectation that we *would* be fasting, and then He went on to explain that we should be cheerful about doing so.

Most people today don't fast regularly. Not on purpose, that is. We are all called upon to give up things sometimes, but very few of us turn those occasions into actual fasts. When we have to sacrifice and don't want to, we either do it to show how noble we are so people can be impressed with us (remind you of anyone we just talked about?), or we do it grudgingly. Rarely do we deliberately offer our fast to God as worship.

Fasting can involve giving up *anything* as an act of worship to God or to devote oneself to prayer. We might give up food, sleep, a particular TV show—any of the things on the list, really. You and I have myriad opportunities daily to fast—to give up something for God's sake. When our child asks for our food, we might choose to give it to her as an offering to Jesus. In other words, we choose to abstain from that food that we were going to eat, and perhaps we offer up a quick prayer: *God, thank You that I have plenty of food— so much, in fact, that I can give some away.* Sacrifice has just become worship, and we have drawn closer to God's heart by talking to Him in prayer.

Or when your baby wakes up in the middle of the night wanting to be fed, you could choose to offer up that time when you'd rather be sleeping as a sacrifice to God. You're going to be up anyway, so you might as well. As you sit there with your baby, you could pray, *God, You know how much I need sleep. But I choose to offer this lack of sleep to You as worship. Thank You for this precious baby and for the opportunity to be here for him/her.* Bingo! You've just turned a negative into a positive.

When you choose to do that—when you choose to offer your sacrifices as fasts to God—you are drawing close to God's heart. You are showing that you are generous like He is and that you submit to His will for your life. You are getting to know Him better as you talk to Him about your sacrifice. Instead of merely making you miserable, your sacrifice is actually helping you grow closer to God. A bite of food or an hour of sleep is a small price to pay for the incredible benefits you reap.

When you sacrifice willingly, you also become more like God. Talk about a Person who sacrifices! God has sacrificed everything imaginable in order to serve us. He even sacrificed Himself in the person of Jesus. Romans 5:8 tells us that "while we were still sinners, Christ died for us." In other words, He died not for people who were acting righteously and loved Him, but for people who were still dead in their sins. Whose actions were unlovely. Who were unlovable, except for the fact that He chose to love us. (Aren't we glad He didn't choose to wait until we were sufficiently lovable before He loved us? If that were the case, we'd still be waiting for His love.)

His crucifixion wasn't the only time Jesus sacrificed Himself for us, however. While He walked this earth, He sacrificed most of those things we listed above—personal space, time alone, His rights, His preferences, and more.

Mark 5:21-43 talks about how Jesus was in the midst of a huge crowd when a man came to Him, begging Him to come and heal his daughter. Jesus went with the man. On the way to his house, someone touched Jesus, and He felt power go out from Him. "Who touched me?" He asked.

Verse 31 says, "And his disciples said to him, 'You see the crowd pressing around you, and yet you say, "Who touched me?"'"

In other words, there were so many people pressing around Jesus that He couldn't even be sure which one of them had touched Him and received healing. Talk about a lack of personal space.

Now let's look at Mark 1:35-39. That day, Jesus got up early in the morning to pray. He knew He needed His own private prayer time. And, as often happens to you and me when we try to get alone with the Father, people went searching for Him. "And Simon and those who were with him searched for him, and they found him and said to him, 'Everyone is looking for you'" (vv. 36-37).

And how about at the very beginning of Jesus' ministry, when He was driven into the wilderness for the devil to tempt Him? (See Matt. 4:1-11.) The Bible tells us that He fasted for 40 days and nights, and that at the end of that time He was hungry. So the devil, knowing good and well that He was hungry, came to Him and tempted Him to satisfy His hunger by turning a stone into bread. Of course, Jesus said no. He was willing to serve God through His fast, even if it meant going hungry.

As a mom, you can understand how Jesus must have felt sometimes when He was asked to sacrifice. He may never have had a child try to find Him while He was in the bathroom, but He understands what it's like to lack privacy. He never had to play a million rounds of Candy Land, but He knows what it's like to spend time with children.

He never sinned, either in attitude or in action, but there must have been times when He was so tired that He longed to sleep rather than keep going. There must have been times when He was so hungry that He wanted to stop and eat but couldn't, or when He just wanted a little time to Himself without people clamoring to be healed or fed. Jesus can identify with us not just because He's God and knows all about us, but because He went through many of the same things we go through. We can identify with Him because we're human too. And when we start identifying with Jesus, we naturally draw closer to His heart and to abundant life.

The Bible tells us in Mark 8:35 that when we are willing to "lose" our lives for Christ's sake, we will "find" them. In other words, if we are willing to lose the life we think is abundant (the one we had all planned out) and take the one God offers (the one that requires sacrifice), we will gain our lives. Mark 8:36-37 goes on to tell us that (I'm paraphrasing here) if we gain everything we thought we wanted and in the process forfeit truly abundant life, that's no good. Instead of seeking all our rights, our food, our clothing, our plans and our sleep, we must be willing to give those things up when called upon in order to gain something much greater: abundant life.

"But how can it be abundant life if I'm always giving things up?" you might ask. That's a reasonable question. But remember that abundant life doesn't consist in our possessions (see Luke 12:15). Abundant life consists in knowing God and becoming like Him. If giving something up helps you to know God and conforms you to His image, then give it up! What you gain is worth far more than what you "lose."

Granted, there are times when it's appropriate to say no to our children. We don't give them everything they ask for, because we know that it's not good for a child never to hear "no" and because some of the things they want aren't good for them. Likewise, there are times when God says no to us, asking us to sacrifice the things we thought we should get, because He knows those things aren't really what we need right now. When we offer our sacrifice to God as an act of worship, submitting willingly to His will, we naturally draw closer to Him. When we turn "missing out" into a deliberate, worshipful fast, we connect with His heart. And again, what do we get when we are close to Him?

Abundant life.

Abundant Living Action Steps

1. List the sacrifices you've made recently for your family. Now offer them to God as worship.
2. What sacrifices do you anticipate being called upon to make in the near future? Offer them as worship in advance.

For a more in-depth study of the topics of each chapter, see the Bible study at the end of this book.

5

Say What?

My mother was a personal friend of God's.
They had ongoing conversations.
DELLA REESE

Children have selective hearing. They can't hear you when you ask them to clean their rooms, but they can sure hear that ice cream truck coming from a mile away. They can't hear you tell them to turn the TV off, but they can hear your head hit the pillow, thereby signaling them to get up out of bed for yet another drink of water. This is why a good portion of training up your children in the way they should go involves teaching them how to listen.

You start by teaching them to pay attention when you're talking to them. If they don't, you call their name again. If they still don't listen, you might have to get down to their level, or step between them and the TV. Next, you teach them to take action based on what they've heard.

The idea is not just to make sure your children physically hear you. The idea is that they both hear what you say and act upon it. When I tell my children to start their bedtime routine, I don't want them just to hear me and understand what I said. I want them to do something about it. Specifically, I want them to clean their rooms, get into their jammies, have their bedtime snack, brush their teeth, and then join me on the couch for family devotions.

This kind of listening—both hearing *and* acting upon what is heard—is the same concept God wants to teach us as His children.

He wants us to hear Him when He speaks to us, and He also wants us to take action—drawing closer to Him, following His instructions, or whatever is appropriate.

Much of the time, we miss what He is saying to us, because we either don't know how to hear Him or we just plain aren't listening. This is unfortunate, because God has a lot to say to us. We've already talked about how we can hear what He has to say through prayer and Bible study. But did you know that there are many other ways in which He speaks to us? Did you realize that He speaks to us all day long, not just when we're sitting somewhere with our Bible open?

Most of us don't hear Him all day long. We figure we're lucky to get five minutes to ourselves to hear from Him before the kids come find us and need something. There's no way we'd ever be able to hear Him all day long, we think.

Oh, but there is, if we just know how to listen.

Listening to God

I'll bet it was easy for Moses to listen to God. After all, Moses heard an actual voice—and he didn't just hear Him once; he heard Him many times. Take the burning bush, for example. Or the time God told Moses to come up onto Mount Sinai to receive the Law (see Exod. 24). Not only that, but God wrote down *with His own finger* exactly what Moses was supposed to do. Kind of hard to be unclear about that.

John the Baptist heard God speak in an audible voice, when He spoke from the cloud at Jesus' baptism (see Matt. 3:17). "This is my beloved Son, with whom I am well pleased," He said.

There are many other examples in the Bible of people who heard God use an audible voice. I have to admit that this has never happened to me. I have never heard an audible voice. I've never seen a burning bush. I've never received stone tablets in my mailbox, instructing: "Thou shalt (fill in the blank)." You probably haven't had any of these things happen to you either.

Does that mean that we can't hear God? Of course not. God knows how to speak to us. He can grab our attention any time He wants. It's a lot easier for Him to do that, though, if we're listening.

So let's talk about four ways we can listen to God.

Listening to God

First, we should make it a point to listen all day long. We already touched on that in an earlier chapter, but it bears repeating. If we only listen at certain times of the day, we're going to miss what God is saying at the other times of the day. Listening doesn't necessarily mean sitting somewhere quietly and trying to hear something, however. It can also involve going throughout our day expectantly, knowing that God could speak at any moment and trying to keep our hearts and ears attuned to Him for when He does speak.

Making it a point to stop at various points during the day and think about what God might want to say to us is a great idea. If we're not purposeful about taking time to listen to God, our ears will be filled with the sounds of society and circumstances, and God's voice will be crowded out. There are many voices clamoring for your attention, and you can't listen to all of them. You make choices each day as to which you will listen to. Do you so fill your ears and mind with other voices that you can't hear God's? Perhaps you could make it a habit, when you sit down to a meal, to stop and think about what God is saying. Perhaps you could do this just before going to bed, or first thing in the morning before getting out of bed. Maybe every time you get into your car, you could stop for a moment and listen for God's voice. Maybe before you turn on the TV, you stop and listen for what God is saying instead of what you're about to hear from Hollywood.

Whenever and wherever you do it, the point is to listen for God's voice all day long, not just at the appointed devotional time. God doesn't confine Himself to speaking only at a certain time of day. We want to be ready to hear Him whenever He chooses to speak.

Second, we need to listen to God instead of our feelings when the two are in conflict. As women, it's easy for us to get caught up in our emotions and to allow them to have too much influence over us. We let them determine our attitudes, thoughts and plans, instead of taking every thought (and emotion!) captive to Christ (see 2 Cor. 10:5). We allow our emotions (instead of God) to determine how we proceed. We *react* instead of *act*.

I'm not suggesting that we ignore our feelings, but rather that when we find ourselves feeling particularly stressed, tired, happy, confused or joyful, we seek to discern how God may be trying to speak to us through them.

Granted, you have to be careful when you do this. If I automatically took each instance of feeling tired as evidence that God wanted me to stay home from church, I'd almost never go. Likewise, if I took every instance of feeling stressed as evidence that I needed more R&R in my life, I'd have way too much R&R. However, if I allow those emotions to prompt me to seek God and ask Him what He might be saying to me, then I have learned to listen to Him through my emotions, instead of letting my emotions run my life.

What difference would it make in your life if, when you felt a negative emotion, you took it before God to see what He might be trying to say to you instead of simply reacting to it? Would your home be more peaceful? Would *you* be more peaceful?

I know it's hard, especially when we're tired or hormonal. But if we learn to use our emotions as prompts to talk to God, we'll be talking to Him a lot more instead of getting stuck in our problems. In other words, we'll experience the abundant life of freedom and peace and knowing Him rather than the meager life we can have when we're overrun by our emotions.

Third, God frequently speaks to us through situations with our children. This has been one of the most fascinating ways of God's speaking that I have ever encountered, and since I learned to hear His voice through these types of situations, a whole new abundant world has opened up to me.

For example, recently I was having a bad day—a reality that was obvious to my children. I made sure to speak to them politely, but I couldn't hide the fact that I was tired and just plain not having a good day. At one point, as I passed through the kitchen, I could see Lindsey in the dining room, busily cutting snowflakes out of printer paper. She had a large pile of fluffy snowflakes sitting on the table in front of her.

As Lindsey heard me come into the dining room, she looked up. Seeing me, she said, "These are for you, Mommy. I know you're having a bad day."

Her love and concern were obvious. But she wasn't the only one who cared about my day; God did too. He had prompted her to do something to try to make me feel better. If I had seen only her heart, I still would have felt better. But seeing God's heart through her actions as well, and knowing that He cared about my day too (though I'll admit I didn't think about it until later), made me feel even better.

But I don't hear God speaking like that, you might be thinking. *How do I do it?*

You can make it a point to think of the spiritual parallels to whatever is going on with you and your children right now. Is your child digging in the front yard? Stop and listen to what God might be saying through that activity. Perhaps He wants to talk to you about searching for Him as you would search for buried treasure.

Or is your child crawling up into your lap, wanting only to be held? Stop and think for a minute. Maybe God is saying to you that He wants you to crawl up into His lap like that and just love on Him—and let Him love on you.

Did your child have a bad day at school and come to you for comfort? Maybe God wants to remind you to come to Him when you need comfort instead of running first to all your girlfriends and a couple of self-help books before you think about Him.

If you stop and think about a particular situation and still aren't sure what God is saying, that's okay. It might take practice to learn to listen to Him in this new way, but it will happen. Remember that He knows how to teach you, and He will do it if you are willing. Just keep making it a point to stop and think. Better yet, stop, think, and talk to God. That's how you'll learn to hear His voice in the everyday stuff of mothering.

Finally, listen to your children's words. Did one child just say something that sounds like it came out of your mouth? Is that a good thing or a bad thing?

Sometimes it may be good, or at least neutral; other times, you may be shocked to hear what your daughter just said to her baby dolls. You may rejoice in the way your child says, "Oh, well. Maybe I'll win next time," or you may cringe at the way he says, "Idiot!" when another driver cuts you off in traffic.

Never forget that your children are learning how to be people from you—and that part of that involves learning how to speak and relate to the world around them. If you hear them saying something just like you that you shouldn't have said either, that's a big clue that God is trying to tell you something.

Maybe one child has spoken rudely to a sibling. Did she learn that tone of voice from you?

I remember once hearing one child say disgustedly to another, "Oh, come on." Before I could discipline the child, the thought flashed into my mind that I had said the same thing many times. Maybe not to that child, but to someone. God's Spirit spoke to my heart right then, saying, "You know how the second child feels right now when the first child said that? You don't want to make your children feel that way when you speak to them, do you?"

Many times, your children's words and tone of voice will be a reflection of yours. At these moments, you might need to hear God's correction. Other times, you'll hear His affirmation that you have done well. In either case, you are listening to Him, and what you hear can help you draw closer to His heart.

That's the purpose of listening to God—not just so that you can do what He says (though certainly that's important), but also

so that you can connect with Him heart to heart. It's pretty difficult to connect intimately with someone you don't listen to.

Many women say that one of the reasons they fell in love with
their husbands was that they had long talks or great conversations
together. Would these same women have fallen in love with the
same men if those men had never listened to them? I doubt it.

Fortunately, God is ready and willing not only to speak to us
all day long as we listen for His voice, but also to listen to us all
day long. He doesn't expect to deliver a monologue that we have
to listen to without responding. He deeply desires to hear from
us too. When you have that kind of back-and-forth, give-and-take
conversation with someone, you get to know him or her. And as
the song says, "To know Him is to love Him." It may sound trite,
but it's true. Knowing God will result in loving Him—and loving
Him, and being in relationship with Him, is what abundant life
is all about.

Once you learn to listen expectantly for God's voice all day
long, to listen to Him instead of to your feelings, and to listen for
His voice in situations with your children and in their words, you'll
begin hearing Him more and more often. You'll discover that He
has more to say to you than you ever knew. And you'll discover
the joy of being constantly in touch with Him—the joy of having
abundant life.

Abundant Living Action Steps

1. Do you know how to listen to God? Rate yourself on a scale of 1-10, with 10 being a great listener. If you don't rate yourself a 10, ask God right now to help you become a better listener.
2. Find a quiet place (I know; it's hard!) to listen to God and spend some time with Him. Ask Him to speak to you and help you to hear what He says.

For a more in-depth study of the topics of each chapter, see the Bible study at the end of this book.

6

Knowing God
Through Worship

*I remember my mother's prayers and they have always followed me.
They have clung to me all my life.*

ABRAHAM LINCOLN

I still remember my daughter Ellie's eighth birthday. It was a Sunday, and after we all ate breakfast, we gathered around the table and presented her gifts to her.

One large bag contained several related gifts—a Nintendo DS Lite and accessories. After many hours of searching, I had found an incredible deal on eBay that put this gift within our financial reach. Ellie had wanted a DS for more than a year, and at eight years old, a year is a long time to want something. I couldn't wait to see the look on her face when she opened her gift.

Ellie removed the tissue paper from the bag and drew out the small, purse-like object (it was the carrying case). She was being very polite, but I could see that she thought it was a purse (which I knew she wouldn't want), and was therefore disappointed. "Open it," I said.

Ellie unzipped the case. She pushed the extra plastic shell aside, not realizing it was a protective accessory for the DS. Then she saw the slim, pink, metallic rectangle. Her jaw dropped and her eyes went wide. For five full seconds, she stood staring in disbelief. Then she shrieked, "It's a DS!"

Let's take a closer look at those few seconds between when Ellie realized what her gift was and when she was able to speak. I want us to do that because her amazed reaction is a perfect illustration of what might happen to us as we worship.

For those brief moments of time, Ellie was breathless with awe, wonder and joy. She was amazed. Her mind and heart were full. Mere words were inadequate to the immensity and intensity of the moment.

That kind of reaction—where we're practically breathless in the face of God's amazing majesty—is truly worshiping God.

Our mind and heart will be full to overflowing. We may or may not use words. If we do, we'll have a sense of how inadequate they are to express the magnitude of God's glory. We'll be consumed by the awe and wonder of His majesty and the immensity of His greatness.

When was the last time you or I worshiped like that? If we can't remember, it's been too long. Please understand that I'm not saying you'll always have the same emotional reaction when you worship, or that your experience of awe in God's presence will look exactly like mine or anyone else's does. But if you never react that way—whatever that looks like for you—you have to wonder if you are really worshiping God on a regular basis.

We desperately need to connect with God spirit to Spirit in worship. We all know that. But actually doing it can be hard. We don't really know what that means, or how to make time to do it. So in this chapter, we'll talk about those things: what true worship looks like, and how we can make sure we make time for it to happen.

But first, let's talk about what true worship isn't. It isn't necessarily a certain physical posture. You might stand or sit while worshiping. You might raise your hands or keep them at your side. You might kneel or even dance. All of these things are okay, and none of them makes a difference, really, except as they express the attitude of your heart. *Posture* does not equal *worship*.

Likewise, worshiping does not have to involve a particular time of day or a particular place. Worship can and does happen anywhere, all over the world, in huts and palaces, outside under shade trees and indoors in inner rooms. It happens morning, noon and night. At any given time of day, there is always someone worshiping God. The time or place you choose to use during your worship time does not determine whether your worship is true.

In the Bible, we're given many examples of people worshiping. Sometimes worship took place in the morning. Sometimes it was at noon, and other times it was at night. Sometimes worship took place inside; sometimes it was outside. Sometimes it was private; sometimes it was corporate. Worship doesn't always have to look the same. Sometimes it will look very different and still be just as true.

Worship is also not a particular formula or set of activities during worship. We attend a church that uses a liturgy, and we love it. We find it beautiful and meaningful and truly helpful to us as we worship God. But that doesn't mean that's the only way to worship. Whether or not your church uses a liturgy, fine. The important thing is that each church must worship God in whatever format seems best to that group of believers.

Similarly, you can find many suggested prayer routines, such as prayer books, devotional books and formulas (such as A.C.T.S. or P.R.A.Y.). Again, the point is not that you use a particular method but that you are *praying*. There's no one right way. All of these resources may be helpful, and they are fine to use. But do not limit yourself to having to worship God a certain way.

The logistics of worship are merely details that should be an outward expression of the worship that is taking place in our hearts. They are not the worship itself. In the heart is where our worship happens.

In fact, the seventh chapter of Acts tells us that the Israelites had been offering sacrifices to God in vain for 40 years, because their hearts weren't in the right place.

We're also told, in Psalm 51:17, about the proper kinds of sacrifice: "The sacrifices of God are a broken spirit; a broken and contrite heart, O God, you will not despise."

Worship is a matter of the heart, not a matter of posture, location, ritual or any other details. It is our heart being right toward

God, and both of our hearts communing together. It's determined not by anything external but by the attitudes of the hearts involved.

So if worship can't be determined by something visible, what does it look like? What's involved? The answer may at first be frustrating. It will then be freeing. The answer is that there's no one right answer.

Louie Giglio defined worship as "our response . . . to God for who He is and what He has done." That is what worship is—not a particular emotion or warm, fuzzy feeling. In fact, if we make the mistake of thinking that our worship will always have a certain emotional quality or intensity, we're setting ourselves up for discouragement. There may or may not be an emotional intensity to our worship. Sometimes there will be; sometimes there won't. That's okay. Just because we haven't felt a certain way doesn't mean we haven't worshiped. If we have presented ourselves before God with a right heart and responded to "who He is and what He has done," we have worshiped. God will teach us more about worshiping as we go along. He may sometimes establish an emotional connection with us that is so deep it leaves us breathless; He may at other times seem more distant, allowing us to worship in truth rather than "in emotion." It's up to Him. Whatever way He chooses is right, and we shouldn't try to make it be something else.

Now, let's talk about how to make time for worship. After all, we're moms. Our schedules are almost always busy, often unpredictable, and occasionally downright crazy. The good news is that even the busiest mom has time for worship. Why? Because we can worship in the midst of our everyday activities. Too often, we think we have to get our activities out of the way so we can have time to connect with God. But the reality is that God wants to connect with us in the midst of our activities. Yes, we should do our best to make space in our schedules for regular one-on-One time with Him. But we also need to learn to worship in the midst of everything that surrounds us.

Five Ways to Worship

One way to do this might be by listening to praise and worship music or hymns as we go about our daily activities. I find music to be very helpful in putting me into a worshipful mood and directing my heart toward God. Plus, it's easy to pop a disc into a CD player or your car and take the music with you wherever you go. You may even find that your children begin to learn the songs you listen to, and that's an added bonus.

Another way to worship throughout the day (and this is something we've already talked about) is to learn to look for the holy— to see God's hand—in the midst of the mundane. Just as Jesus often used ordinary things like harvests, seeds and sheep to show Himself to His listeners, so too God today uses the ordinary stuff of our lives like laundry, diapers and dishes to communicate His truth to us. If we wait until the house is calm and quiet to recognize God's presence, we're cutting Him out of a huge portion of our day. He wants to communicate with us all day long. If we don't watch for Him all day long, we're missing out.

A third way to worship in the midst of it all is to offer our work as service to God. After all, Jesus said that whatever we do for "the least of these," we do for Him. Check it out:

When the Son of Man comes in his glory, and all the angels with him, then he will sit on his glorious throne. Before him will be gathered all the nations, and he will separate people one from another as a shepherd separates the sheep from the goats. And he will place the sheep on his right, but the goats on the left. Then the King will say to those on his right, "Come, you who are blessed by my Father, inherit the kingdom prepared for you from the foundation of the world. For I was hungry and you gave me food, I was thirsty and you gave me drink, I was a stranger and you welcomed me, I was naked and you clothed me, I was sick and you visited me, I was in prison and you came to me." Then the righteous will answer him, saying, "Lord, when did we see you hungry and feed you, or thirsty and give you drink? And when did we see you a stranger and welcome you, or naked and clothe you? And when did we see you sick or in prison and visit you?" And the King will answer them, "Truly, I say to you, as you did it to one of the least of these my brothers, you did it to me."

Then he will say to those on his left, "Depart from me, you cursed, into the eternal fire prepared for the devil and his angels. For I was hungry and you gave me no food, I was thirsty and you gave me no drink, I was a stranger and you did not welcome me, naked and you did not clothe me, sick and in prison and you did not visit me." Then they also will answer, saying, "Lord, when did we see you hungry or thirsty or a stranger or naked or sick or in prison, and did not minister to you?" Then he will answer them, saying, "Truly, I say to you, as you did not do it to one of the least of these, you did not do it to me." And these will go away into eternal punishment, but the righteous into eternal life (Matt. 25:31-46).

So if we're doing laundry, we can stand there, sorting our children's dirty clothes, and pray, "Jesus, I'm offering this service to You. You ask us to worship You with all we have, and right now, what I have is laundry. So I offer it to You from a willing heart." See? We've worshiped in the midst of laundry.

Or perhaps as we set a meal on the table, we offer it to God as His meal. "God, I place this meal before my family and before You as my offering to You tonight. Thank You, God, that You receive this humble offering."

You can turn even the most humdrum daily tasks of mothering into an opportunity to worship God by offering your service directly to Him. The truly amazing thing is that He will receive those acts of service as done to Him personally, not just done to your family!

A fourth way to worship is to cultivate a heart attitude of listening so that we *can* hear Him. Probably the biggest chunk of our day is spent not really thinking about God. The second largest amount of time (though it's a far smaller amount) is usually spent talking to God. In far distant third, if we do it at all, is the time we spend listening to God. I know it's hard to listen without becoming distracted. But we don't necessarily have to stay quiet and focused for long blocks of time. In fact, God will sometimes direct our wandering thoughts to areas He wants us to meditate on before Him or pray about. And if we practice focusing on Him, we'll get better at doing it more frequently and for longer periods of time when necessary.

My husband enjoys telling me about his day at work, and I enjoy hearing about it. But the reason I enjoy it is not just because I think what he has to say is interesting. It's also because I'm glad for the opportunity to listen to my husband—to show him that I love him by listening to what he wants to say. In the same way, we can show God that we love Him by listening to Him—if we do it with a willing heart, that is, and not just because we think we have to. God loves to know that we want to listen to Him—that we're not just doing it out of obligation.

A fifth way to worship is to reflect back to God who and how amazing we know Him to be. I enjoy hearing compliments; I'm sure you do too. We know that even God does, because we're told in Scripture that He formed Israel so that they could declare His praise (see Isa. 43:21). He is no less desirous of our praise today. Over and over in Scripture, in both the Old and New Testaments, God's people are commanded to praise and thank Him. God likes to receive our praise and gratitude. He loves hearing what we think of Him and His actions. Don't you love it when one of your children throws her arms around you and says, "Mommy, you're the greatest"? Of course you do. So God loves it when you—His child—do the same thing.

Worship is not complicated. At least it doesn't have to be. All we need to do is present ourselves before God and respond to Him. If you don't know whether to start your worship time by praying, reading your Bible, remaining silent, or some other activity, ask Him. He'll tell you. Remember that the main thing is not what you do, but the fact that you are offering God your heart. You can do that anytime and anywhere. Because wherever and whenever you are, He'll find you and meet you—and worship will happen. When it does . . . well, that, my friend, is abundant life.

Abundant Living Action Steps

1. How do you worship God best? In what kind of surroundings? Make plans right now for a time when you can go to that place and spend some worship time with Him.
2. What do you like to do to worship God? How can you incorporate that into your day today?

For a more in-depth study of the topics of each chapter, see the Bible study at the end of this book.

Shhhhhh

We need to find God, and he cannot be found in noise and restlessness.
God is the friend of silence. See how nature—trees, flowers,
grass—grows in silence; see the stars, the moon and the sun,
how they move in silence. . . . We need silence to be able to touch souls.

MOTHER TERESA

Our house can get pretty loud and crazy at times. I bet yours can too. Whether the noise comes from your baby screaming, your kids chasing each other through the house while they're supposed to be getting ready for bed, or any of the myriad toys and games they have that all make noise, life with kids is sometimes loud. Very loud.

I remember once having to shout nearly at the top of my lungs in order to be heard over the sounds of my kids' voices and playing. Once they realized I was trying to get their attention, they became quiet. They also looked a little confused. "Why are you shouting, Mommy?" they asked.

Kids may not know how loud they are, but you and I know. We also know what it's like to long for just a little bit of quiet. For just a few minutes, even. For example, as I was working on this chapter, the phone rang. It was my husband, who is out of town with our children at his parents' home, so I answered it.

Almost immediately, I heard my children's voices begin to shout into the phone (he had it on speaker), telling me all about their day. Lindsey had gotten a bruise, and Ellie had a carpet burn. As far as I could tell, Jessica and Kenny were fine. I listened to them talk, not understanding most of what they said, until my husband shooed them away from the phone and said it was time for bed.

I understand why, on first hearing about the idea of "silence" or "quietness" as a way of getting to know God, you may very well be tempted to respond, "Wouldn't that be nice—but it'll never happen!"

It would, indeed, be nice. And it *can* happen. It's not only nice, but also possible. Maybe not as much silence as we'd like, and maybe not at the times we'd like. But if we desire to make silence a part of our walk with God, there are ways to make it happen.

Before we talk about those ways, let's answer the question "Why silence?" What's the point?

The point of silence in this context is to hear God speak. When we are constantly talking, listening to the radio, or watching TV, God doesn't have room to get a word in edgewise. Sure, He could raise His voice and drown out all the other voices we're listening to. He could even do something more spectacular, like set a bush on fire. But why would we want to so clog up our ears with all the other things we're listening to that God has to do something drastic just for us to hear Him?

I guarantee you . . . we don't. If our lives are so busy and so loud that God has to shout to get our attention, that's a situation we don't want to be in.

In fact, the Bible commands us to seek times of silence or stillness. Psalm 37:7 says, "Be still before the LORD and wait patiently for him; fret not yourself over the one who prospers in his way, over the man who carries out evil devices!"

Psalm 46:10 says, "Be still, and know that I am God. I will be exalted among the nations, I will be exalted in the earth!"

And check out Mark 6:31: "Then, because so many people were coming and going that they did not even have a chance to eat, he said to them, 'Come with me by yourselves to a quiet place and get some rest'" (*NIV*).

Fortunately, quietness is not limited to a particular hour or location. But we do have to carve out time for it if we want to experience it. If we're not purposeful about it, the voices of this world (including our own voice!) will rush in to fill the silence. In order for quietness and silence to happen, we have to tune out the other voices competing for our attention. I'd like to suggest three voices we can tune out if we want to focus on hearing God's voice.

Three Voices We May Need to Silence

First, we can silence our own voice. Even if we're not especially talkative by nature, there's a lot of speaking we have to do in order to run a household. What if, instead of talking our way through the day, we tried to see how few words we could get by with? If all day won't work, maybe we can practice this for shorter periods of time. Perhaps some days, instead of calling a friend, we could choose to be silent for a few minutes. Maybe instead of chatting at the dinner table, we could choose to listen to our family talk instead, with an ear tuned to hear what God might say to us through their conversation. We might be surprised at what we heard if we listened instead of talked.

I'm sure you can think of ways you can silence your voice that will work particularly well for you in your circumstances. You probably can't go 24 hours without talking. But even if it's five minutes, that's five minutes more than what you would have had otherwise.

In those five minutes of silence, listen to God. Maybe He will speak to you during this time. Maybe He will make you aware of something you didn't previously know. Maybe He will cause you to see things in a different light. Whatever He chooses to do with your gift of silence, it will be worthwhile.

I remember a time when I was trying to work out how to do something difficult. I had turned the problem every which way in my mind, and I didn't know how to proceed. "Let it be for a while," my Aunt Susan advised me, "and go do something to relax. Take your mind off of it."

"But I want to get this figured out," I protested.

"Let it be," she repeated. "It may be that during your time of quiet, God will show you what to do about it."

So after she prayed with me, I left the computer and went to soak in a long, hot bath. As I lay there in the water, I tried not to think about anything in particular. Then, suddenly, I knew how to proceed with what I had been trying to accomplish.

But it's only been five minutes, I thought to myself. *I should take more quiet time than that.*

It's true that on most occasions, I do need more than five minutes to resolve an issue. But this particular time, God turned my thoughts in just the right direction so that in only a few minutes, I was ready to get back to work.

I accomplished in five minutes of quietness what might have taken me hours to hammer out otherwise, thanks to God's help. You see, quietness is not for worship alone. It's also an opportunity for God to speak into your frenzied life and help you out.

A secondary benefit of silence is that it gives us a chance to calm ourselves down from our stress, worries, anger or anxiety. As women, we often like to talk things out in order to solve them, and that's fine. It's the way God made us. But He also made us for times of silence, during which we just keep quiet and reflect as we listen for His voice. I wonder how many of our "emergencies" or "vitally important crises" would become less important or maybe even disappear altogether if we took time to be silent about them. I don't know about you, but a life with fewer crises and less stress sounds pretty "abundant" to me.

In times of need, most of us call a friend (or, nowadays, text or instant message a friend) before we take quiet time with God. On one hand, this is understandable, because we are made for relationships with others, and it's easy to tell what others are saying and to receive help from them. But on the other hand, we miss a tremendous opportunity by not turning to God first and asking Him to assist us. The problem is that either we don't think of going to Him or we don't trust Him to help us out with our problems. If only we would get used to taking quiet time before Him and listening for His voice first, we'd find out just how helpful He is longing to be.

Second, we can silence media voices. Most of us spend far more time listening to music or playing around on the computer

(Facebook, anyone?) than we do being silent and listening for God's voice. Instead of playing our favorite online game, why not take those minutes and listen for God? Why not turn the radio off during our daily commute and listen to God instead of a DJ? True, it's hard to get away from media input. But we have far more control over how much media we allow into our lives than we think we do. Media voices are not necessarily bad in and of themselves. But anything that steals time that would be better spent with God should be reduced or eliminated.

Any time we take away from media and devote to God can only be for our benefit. What would we hear if we spent as much time listening to Him and seeking Him as we do on our media pursuits? I know my life would be a lot quieter, and yours probably would be too.

Third, we can teach our children to keep their voices silent at times. Believe me, I know how hard it is for kids to be quiet. But even young children can be taught to be silent for one minute when Mommy tells them she is listening to God. The length of time you instruct them to allow you to be silent can be gradually increased as they get older. Obviously, if they have a legitimate need, you would tend to them and have your time of silence later. But it's also a need for children to see their mother honoring the Lord and seeking to hear His voice above all others. I guarantee that if you tell your children you are talking to God and they must be quiet, they will become curious. They may ask you what you're praying about, and you might decide to tell them. You could also invite them to establish a prayer time of their own, or perhaps they would be curious enough about your time that they would come up with the idea of a personal prayer time independently.

Even if they don't—even if they run off and play—you still win. You have your quiet time with God, and you've set a good example for your kids. You have your abundant life, and you've shown your children one way they can have it too. There's not much that's more powerful in causing kids to seek God than a mother's example.

Once you decide to make silence happen, and you actually follow through on achieving silence for a brief instant, your thoughts may very well wander. It's hard to keep focused when you don't hear anything going on. But by repeatedly bringing your thoughts back to the subject at hand—God—you can train yourself to stay focused in silence for longer periods of time. I'm not nearly as good at this yet as I'd like to be; my thoughts wander easily. Fortunately, I have help in learning to be quiet before God—the same help that is available to you. God will help me train myself to be silent yet actively waiting on Him, and He'll help you too. It will take time and practice. God probably won't bestow the ability to concentrate upon us all at once. But He will make our practice effective.

You might want to keep a pencil and paper handy to write down things that come to your mind while you are having your time with God. That way, when something pops into your mind that might be important, you don't have to try to remember it. You can simply write it down and know it's there to be referred to later.

God may not speak to us every time we wait silently before Him, but even so, that time is never wasted. It's good training for future silence to come. In addition, it shows God that we're serious about wanting to hear from Him—so serious that we're willing to eliminate even some of our favorite distractions. That blesses His heart. After all, how would we feel if our children came to us and said, "Mommy, I'm just going to stay here and be quiet for as long as I can, or until you speak. I don't want to miss anything you have to say. Your voice is what I most want to hear"?

Okay, to tell the truth, we'd probably be shocked. But the point is that just as we long for our children to want to listen to us, so too God longs to have us wait before Him to hear Him if He chooses to speak.

Imagine being the mother of 10 children. That's right, 10. Susanna Wesley was such a mother. With that many children (9 more had died in infancy, by the way), she certainly didn't have much time to sit silently before God. So what did she do? When she wanted time to talk to God, she would sit in her chair and pull her apron up over her head, hiding her face. She trained her children to know that when Mommy was under her apron talking to God, they were not to disturb her. She found her quiet place in the midst of the noise and chaos of raising that many children. You and I can certainly find time and space for quietness in our homes too.

Being silent before God shows Him how important He is to us. It gives Him joy. In the sweet communion we'll have with Him—or even just the delight of being in His presence—our hearts will be glad too. And our lives will be abundant.

Abundant Living Action Steps

1. What voices do you need to silence in order to hear from God? Name a specific time when you can silence those voices and listen to Him.
2. Try silencing your own voice and thoughts for a few moments right now. What does God have to say to you?

For a more in-depth study of the topics of each chapter, see the Bible study at the end of this book.

8

Giving

As a mother I think you often get so caught up in trying to take care of everyone else that you forget to take care of yourself.

MIA HAMM

At first glance, "giving" might not seem like a topic in which moms need instruction. We spend our lives giving—anytime, anywhere, with or without advance notice. What more could we possibly need to learn?

The kind of giving we usually think about involves giving of ourselves—in other words, sacrifice, as we discussed in a previous chapter. The kind of giving we're going to discuss in this chapter involves giving not just of ourselves but also of our resources.

Fear not! I'm not going to say we should simply find a way to give more. I'm not going to place yet another burden on our overworked backs. Instead, I'll help us look at what the Bible says about giving, which will actually lighten the load of the giving we are called to do and transform our giving from drudgery into worship.

Matthew 10:8—an oft-quoted verse about giving—comes at the end of a list of things Jesus was commanding His followers to do as He sent them out. Let's look at the whole passage for context:

He called his twelve disciples to him and gave them authority to drive out evil spirits and to heal every disease and sickness. These are the names of the twelve apostles: first, Simon (who is called Peter) and his brother Andrew; James son of Zebedee, and his brother John; Philip and

Bartholomew; Thomas and Matthew the tax collector; James son of Alphaeus, and Thaddaeus; Simon the Zealot and Judas Iscariot, who betrayed him. These twelve Jesus sent out with the following instructions: "Do not go among the Gentiles or enter any town of the Samaritans. Go rather to the lost sheep of Israel. As you go, preach this message: 'The kingdom of heaven is near.' Heal the sick, raise the dead, cleanse those who have leprosy, drive out demons. Freely you have received, freely give" (Matt. 10:1-8, *NIV*).

"Go do all this stuff for people," Jesus said. Then He gave His disciples the reason they should do so: "Freely you have received, freely give."

In other words, Jesus was reminding the disciples that everything they had, including the power to do these miracles, they had received freely from Him. Therefore, He told them, since you have received so many things freely, turn around and give freely to others.

We're going to discuss giving freely to others, but before we do that, we need to talk about the first part of Jesus' statement: "Freely you have received." We must learn how to receive freely, or we won't have anything to give. Let's look at three things we need to know how to receive from God.

Receiving from God

The first, of course, is salvation. Receiving salvation from God is the foundation for everything else we do as Christians, and not just because it is what makes us Christians. Let's look at what salvation is and why it is so foundational.

Being "saved" means that in Jesus' death on the cross, where He took the punishment for the sins of the world, He also took the punishment for our sins. You are a sinner. So am I. Our sins separated us so vastly far from God that we had no hope of ever being reconciled to Him (and no desire to be, either). The punishment we justly deserved for our sins was death (see Rom. 6:23), but Jesus took that punishment so that we didn't have to. Now, His complete and perfect righteousness takes the place of our sinfulness, so that when God looks at us, He sees not all of our mess-ups, but the perfection of Jesus. It's amazing, isn't it, that God would sacrifice Himself to save us, who didn't deserve it?

But that's exactly what happened, and if we don't understand this, we are missing out on the foundational truth of being a Christian—that Christ made a way for us to be reconciled to God. He opened up for us a whole new relationship with our Maker and an abundant life filled with every spiritual blessing (see Eph. 1:3).

Although this gift cost Jesus His life, it doesn't cost us anything. So that's one way in which we have freely received. We have freely received Jesus, so we should freely share the great news that others can have a relationship with Him too. Anybody who wants to, in fact. Out of our immense gratitude for this incredible gift, we should be willing to share it with others.

Second, we have freely received God's provision for our needs, both material and spiritual. In Philippians 4:19, Paul assures us, "And my God will meet all your needs according to his glorious riches in Christ Jesus." In context, this verse is not talking merely about spiritual needs, but about very real physical needs as well. God will indeed supply what we need for daily living—and not grudgingly, either. He's glad to do it. He loves to meet our needs.

As moms, you and I are glad to supply our children's needs for food and clothing. Why would we think God would be any less glad to meet our needs? Yet sometimes we get caught up in the idea that God only meets our needs out of some sense of obligation or duty. This is far from the truth! Remember Malachi 3:10, which says that if we trust God to take care of us and do our part, He will shower blessings upon us so great that we won't even have room to receive them all? *That's* the truth. God loves to give and is ready to do so abundantly.

Sometimes I get worn out from giving. Burned out. Stressed out. Occasionally even resentful. But God never does. He continues to give freely, out of His free will, and to shower blessings upon us. Just as He has freely met our needs, so too we are to be willing freely to meet the needs of others. (We'll talk more about what this looks like later on in this chapter.)

So we've received salvation (the greatest blessing of all), and we've received provision for all our needs. But there's another category of thing we have received, and that's extra blessings. Blessings above and beyond what we need. Blessings of luxuries that aren't necessary.

We may not be rich according to American standards (though we're still far richer than hundreds of millions—maybe even billions—of people in many countries in the world). But even if we're living paycheck to paycheck, we still enjoy many things that aren't strictly necessary for our survival. Do we ever get to eat out? That's not necessary. Do we have a computer in our home? That's not necessary, either. True, this is a very technological age, but we could use the computers at the library. Do we have more than one car, or more than two sets of clothes, or a pantry and refrigerator full of food? Then we've received extra blessings.

God's not obligated to give us as many things as He does. The only things He's obligated to give us as our Father are those things that are necessary for our survival until we've completed His purpose on earth. The fact that He has chosen to give us so many extras means that we have freely received far more than we likely have ever thought about.

So, then, if we have freely received, we are to freely give. We're going to look at three people or groups of people to whom we are to give. But first, let me tell you a story.

Recently, my son Kenny lost his Nintendo 3DS. The whole family looked everywhere for it, but we couldn't find it. My husband, Phil, sat Kenny down and explained that Kenny would have to earn the money to buy another one. Kenny tried hard not to cry, but, faced with the possibility of not having a 3DS for a really long time, the tears began to fall.

Seeing him so sad and realizing what was going on, Jessica went into her room and came back out holding something. She went over to Kenny and opened her hand. In her palm were a dollar and a quarter—all the money she had. "Here, Kenny," she said. "Here's money for your DS."

That's just the kind of caring person Jessica is. She's all about giving freely, even if it means she has nothing left. If she has something that can meet someone else's need, she'll give it to them, even if it grieves her to do so.

But that's not the end of the story. Later that day, our family attended a party celebrating the baptism of our neighbor's son. We enjoyed the food, music, fellowship and fun. There were activities for the kids. One activity involved one of the adults throwing handfuls of candy into the air while the kids scrambled to gather it up. Jessica wanted some of the candy, but at five years old and tending toward shyness, she was intimidated by all the scrambling for candy. She wound up with only one piece because she wasn't comfortable diving for the candy like the other kids (including the rest of mine).

When we got home, her siblings all began to spread out their candy and eat it, but Jessica began to cry. She was sad that she had only one piece while everyone else had what seemed like a million pieces. While I comforted her, Phil bent down next to Kenny and whispered something into his ear.

The way Phil tells it, he reminded Kenny of the generous sacrifice Jessica had made for him earlier. "Why don't you give her some of your candy," he suggested.

Phil said he could see the wheels turning in Kenny's head as Kenny's remembrance of Jessica's generosity warred with his desire to keep all his candy for himself. Fortunately, love and gratitude for his sister won out, and he shared. Just as he had freely received, so too he freely gave.

Jessica properly thanked him. We need to realize going into a giving situation, though, that we're not always going to be thanked for what we do. As human beings, we like to be acknowledged for our actions. We like to be noticed, appreciated and thanked. Most businesses understand this, so they develop ways to show their employees the desired affirmation. Notice here that it's not necessarily the clients or customers who express appreciation; it's usually the bosses who deem an employee's performance exemplary and worthy of gratitude.

This is how being a mom works too. We don't often get thanks from our "customers" either, unless it's an obligatory thank-you when we tell them they forgot to say it. But our "boss"—God Himself!—is constantly offering us encouragement, thanks and praise. He's told us over and over in Scripture how much He loves us and values us. He's promised that He will help us with whatever we need. He's even guaranteed that our work is *not* in vain! (See 1 Cor. 15:58.) He's made Himself available 24/7 whenever we want to talk to Him, and He doesn't mind that it might be in the midst of making supper or cleaning the oven. He's told us that He delights in us. He's even said that He is—get this—pleased with our sacrifices.

So while we may not hear thanks from the people to whom we give, God is always thankful for our gifts and has made sure to tell us so.

The fact remains, though, that giving to God often involves giving not to Him directly, but to those He cares about. In other words, human beings. Let's start with talking about giving to our family.

Giving to Others

It's easy to delight in giving things like Christmas and birthday presents. Those things are fun. But what about the boring things? The mundane?

We give breakfast, lunch and dinner. We give new socks and underwear. We give rides to places our children want to go. We give privileges.

Yes, our children may need to fulfill certain responsibilities in order to be taken places or earn some of these privileges. But for the most part, we give things like this with no strings attached. In fact, all the things our children have have been given to them—by us or by someone else.

The question is: Do we give these good gifts freely or grudgingly?

In our family, when I've just bought something at the store, like groceries or new school clothes, I often offer an out-loud prayer on the way home: "Thank You, God, for the money to buy these things. Thank You that You always provide for us."

I want our kids to learn that the things they receive don't just come from Mommy and Daddy; ultimately, they come from God. And I want them to see me meeting their needs in the same way God does—freely and willingly.

Giving to those outside the family is important too. No matter your economic situation, there is always someone less fortunate than you who could benefit from your money, or things you might buy them, or things you don't need anymore that are still in good condition, or even your time. If you think you don't have enough to be able to give anything to anybody else, you're mistaken.

You have received freely from God, and one of the reasons this is the case is so that you can give freely to others—whether to people you know or people you don't. If you hang onto all your possessions (or all your money) because they're "yours," you're denying somebody the blessing God meant for them to have.

Granted, it can be tricky to decide when and to whom to give. Just because you have money or extra items you don't need doesn't mean you can or should give to every need you are aware of. You will have to be purposeful and prayerful in discerning which of others' needs to meet, and which to leave for God to fulfill in some other way. You want to give your resources when and to whom God says to give. So when an opportunity to give comes your way, prayerfully consider it. Then give as God leads you.

When we hold our resources in a loose hand and distribute them freely as God directs, we draw closer to His heart. We learn to see needs with His eyes. We learn that abundant life consists not just in having, but also in giving.

Of course, giving is easier if we have been living frugally, and we'll discuss that in the next chapter.

Abundant Living Action Steps

1. Have you received the three things we have the opportunity to receive from God? If you haven't received salvation, why wait? Ask Him for it now.
2. What do you have that God may want you to give to others? Make specific plans to give what He leads you to give.

For a more in-depth study of the topics of each chapter, see the Bible study at the end of this book.

9

Frugality

I want my children to have all the things I couldn't afford.
Then I want to move in with them.
PHYLLIS DILLER

What comes to your mind when you hear the word "frugal"? I'll admit that for me, "frugal" used to connote "miserly" or "cheap." Now, however, it means something far more and far better. That's because I've learned that frugality is a way to bring blessings not only to my own family but also to others. Even better, it brings glory to God. In this chapter, we'll look at what frugality means, why it's so important, and how it can lead to abundant life. (For the purposes of this chapter, I'm going to define "frugality" as "living within one's means." In other words, it means living on whatever money and resources God has provided us.)

Explaining frugality to kids can be hard. I remember a time when I told Ellie (then five years old) that we didn't have enough money for a particular item. She suggested that we simply go to the ATM and get some more money. I explained that the ATM only gives you the money that you have put into the bank, and that eventually, you run out. "Oh," she said, disappointed.

Money, like all other earthly resources, is not unlimited. God has allowed each of us to be stewards of a certain amount of those resources. If we misuse the resources He has entrusted to us, or tie them up in things that are of secondary importance, we won't have the ability to pursue things that are of primary significance.

Let's state the obvious first. If we're buying luxuries like fash-ionable new clothes and restaurant meals on credit because we want them but can't afford them, we're living beyond the means God has chosen to give us. The writer of Hebrews tells us, "Keep your lives free from the love of money and be content with what you have, because God has said, 'Never will I leave you; never will I forsake you'" (Heb. 13:5, *NIV*).

But many of us don't live the way this verse instructs us to. Having new or luxurious things is more important to us than showing both God and a watching world that we are content with what He's provided and really don't need more. We would never tell God directly that we feel like He hasn't provided enough, but our actions and spending habits show that that's what we believe.

Frugality is a way to show God and the world that we're content with what He's provided. It doesn't just mean not buying things we can't really afford; it also means not living right at the edge of our means, so we can have a little financial breathing room. Most Americans live paycheck to paycheck, spending every last dime before the next one comes along. True, it can be challenging to live any other way when there are so many things we'd like to buy, have and do, and when "everyone else" is living this way. But do we really need to spend everything we make? Has God really provided barely enough for our needs so that we can't even save a dime?

Now let me say that I know that some of us are on extremely tight budgets, and the fact that we're even making it from one paycheck to the next is a testimony to our budgetary skills. That's not the kind of situation I'm talking about. I'm talking about when we have enough for our needs, but we spend every extra penny on luxuries instead of trying to save anything at all, so that when something unexpected comes along, we don't have any resources from which to deal with it.

What a testimony it would be to a watching world if we showed by our financial decisions that God has provided enough for us and that we trust Him to continue to do so in the future! Learning to live in this kind of trust in God is abundant life, my friends. We don't have to worry about whether or not God will provide. In fact, Jesus tells us

> And do not seek what you are to eat and what you are to drink, nor be worried. For all the nations of the world seek after these things, and your Father knows that you need them. Instead, seek his kingdom, and these things will be added to you.... For where your treasure is, there will your heart be also (Luke 12:29-31,34).

Where is your treasure? Is it in all the things you can buy, or is it in the fact that God has provided for you and that you know He will continue to do so every day of your life?

Blessings Frugality Brings

In addition to bringing glory to God, frugality also brings blessings to us, our families and other people. It's a huge blessing for a family to live within their means. Statistics tell us that the number one thing couples fight about is money. If a family lives within their means, three things will happen.

First, Mom and Dad aren't as likely to be stressed and fighting about money. It's tough on the kids when Mom and Dad fight, no matter what it's about. So if money is always a concern, and Mom and Dad are always fighting about it, guess who's always going to be stressed? Yep—the kids. Frugality, on the other hand, or living within one's means, means that Mom and Dad won't have money issues to fight about, and that takes a huge stressor off of them, their marriage and the entire family.

Second, when a family chooses to live within its means, children learn to be content with what they have. If Mom and Dad are always grumbling about what they don't have, kids learn to do the same. In contrast, when Mom and Dad are content with what they have and don't always feel the need to obtain the newest car or gadget, kids learn the same thing.

True, it's not fun to have to tell the kids they can't have something because the family can't afford it. And I'm not suggesting that the parents burden the children with the family's financial problems. But when the family can't afford something, the parents can explain it to the children in a way that leaves the children marveling at God's goodness instead of feeling resentful that they can't have what they want.

For example, parents could say, "We can't afford that right now, but look at all the amazing things you do have." In this way, the parents are reframing their refusal to buy the item in a positive way—in terms of God's goodness. They're also teaching their children to look at the positive side of things instead of the negative. They're teaching their kids that abundant life lies not in getting more things, but in enjoying what God's already been graciously good to give us.

Third, when a family practices frugality, everybody enjoys the freedom to save up money for special purchases instead of having to scare up some money to pay the bills for purchases that have already been enjoyed. Buying things on credit might seem like a good idea or even the only option, but believe me, there is a choice. That choice involves doing without, which is why so many of us don't choose it.

We get this idea in our heads that only with the thing we can't afford could we be truly happy or content, and so we buy the thing because doing so is less stressful than denying ourselves. But what difference would it make if we reframed it like this: "God hasn't given me the money for that right now, so I must not really need it. Thanks, God, for what I already have."

We'd move a lot closer to experiencing our life as abundant the way it already is, instead of thinking we have to have more and more in order to be happy.

Jesus once instructed His disciples to do without and wait and watch for Him to provide: "He told them: 'Take nothing for the journey—no staff, no bag, no bread, no money, no extra tunic'" (Luke 9:3, *NIV*).

Was Jesus sending His disciples out into the world unprepared? At first glance, it would seem so. But remember, Jesus knew that God would provide for them. Jesus sent them out like this so that they could learn to experience God's provision. If they had taken plenty of food and money, and suitcases full of stuff, they might never have had to learn to rely on God for supply.

Likewise, God sometimes asks us to do without so that He can teach us to rely on Him instead of on our own resources. My husband recently became aware of a job opening in his company for which he felt particularly suited. The new position, if he got it, would provide a better schedule and allow Phil more time to be at home with us. In addition, it would be the kind of work that he would like to do. It would feel much more like ministry to him than his current job did (though of course we know that ministry can be done in any position, anywhere). The only drawback to this amazing job was that it would pay significantly less money.

My husband and I spent a lot of time talking and praying about whether he should accept the job if he was offered it. We prayed about it before and during his interview, and then after his interview while he waited to hear if he got the job. Ultimately, we came to the conclusion that God wanted us to be willing to accept the marvelous new job, even though it paid quite a bit less. So we determined that if he was offered it, he would accept.

Then, the rubber met the road. Phil was chosen from among the candidates and offered the job. Now came the real test: Would we accept what we believed God wanted for us, knowing that it would significantly impact our budget, or would we decide that he should stay in his current position and continue to make more money?

We joyfully accepted the job, and God has already made it abundantly clear in a variety of ways that we did the right thing. If our eyes had been merely on the bottom line, we would have settled for more money but less than God's best. As it is, our family can look forward to this new position and enjoy my husband and their father being at home with us more. If we can't buy a few of the extras we bought before, that's okay. The abundant life God has planned for our family doesn't consist in our possessions.

Living within our means not only blesses our own family, but it also helps bless others financially. How does that work? One possibility is that we might have money saved up to share with others when something unexpected (or even expected) comes up. It's a special blessing to be able to take some of our money and use it for others' benefit. It's a great way to teach kids generosity. Perhaps we can even let the children help choose how a portion of the available funds will be used to benefit others. When our children see us using the family's money to help others, they will learn to hold their possessions a little more loosely themselves. Who knows? Maybe when they are older, they will remember our example and give to others from the resources God has provided their new family.

Another possibility is that we might have money to give to others because we don't need it for interest payments (which are roughly the equivalent of throwing money down a hole) or to make payments on things we've bought for ourselves. When we tie up our money in buying things for ourselves, whether making charge card payments or simply buying things outright, we leave less money available to bless others.

Have you ever had something come up or heard of a need where you really wished you could help out? You might have been able to, if you'd been saving up some of your money and keeping it free from other obligations. Most of us can save at least a dollar or two per paycheck. If we're not doing that, it's usually because we don't want to or haven't thought about it.

If a situation comes up, and we can't give much, but can only give a little, that's okay. Mark 12:41-44 says this:

Jesus sat down opposite the place where the offerings were put and watched the crowd putting their money into the temple treasury. Many rich people threw in large amounts. But a poor widow came and put in two very small copper coins, worth only a fraction of a penny. Calling his disciples to him, Jesus said, "I tell you the truth, this poor widow has put more into the treasury than all the others. They all gave out of their wealth; but she, out of her poverty, put in everything—all she had to live on" (*NIV*).

So God is pleased with whatever you give. After all, He is the one who has provided all your resources. He's not going to penalize you for not being able to give what He never gave you in the first place. As it says in 2 Corinthians 8:12, "For if the readiness is there, it is acceptable according to what a person has, not according to what he does not have."

Now, lest you think I'm saying that our family handles money perfectly, let me assure you that that is not the case. I'm speaking to myself in this chapter just as much as I am to you. There are financial decisions we have made in the past that I would change if I could. There have been times we gave or didn't give, or purchases we made, that I would re-do, if given the opportunity. But our overall trend (especially lately) has been to try to be good stewards of the money God has given us and to live within our means.

I'm also not saying that emergencies will never arise and you will never have to put anything on a credit card. If a member of my family had sudden, significant medical expenses and we had to charge those, I'd do it, and I wouldn't feel bad about it. I'm not talking about when we've been doing the best we can with our money and something happens to push us over the top and down the other side of the hill. I'm talking about when we deliberately buy unnecessary items that we can't afford, when there is no emergency in sight.

God doesn't ask us to be good stewards of our money so that He can take all the fun out of life. He doesn't ask for frugality so that He can deprive us of material possessions that would be good for us. He asks us to live within our means so that we can learn to trust Him and His provision, so that we can bless others, and so that we can be blessed ourselves. Frugality should be a joy. Look at all the abundant blessings it leads to!

Abundant Living Action Steps

1. Do you rely more on God or on your own resources? Make a list of the resources God has given you. Go to Him in prayer and thank Him for each of them, telling Him that you know that they are gifts from Him.
2. Which blessing of frugality seems most desirable to you? Make a list of any ways you need to be more frugal so that you can enjoy that blessing.

For a more in-depth study of the topics of each chapter, see the Bible study at the end of this book.

10

Fellowship

Fellowship with like-minded believers is an
essential element in God's Church.
Pamela Rose Williams

For a few years, I belonged to a small Hispanic congregation, where I served as youth minister. Though the youth activities were in English, the other services were in Spanish. I speak Spanish, so that worked fine for me. I loved being a member there. The people were warm and welcoming, and everything was so much fun. I got to live and move in a culture different from my own; and even better than that, I had the privilege of being part of this particular body of believers, who loved and supported one another.

One of my favorite church activities was when we would have a *compañerismo*—a "fellowship." This usually took place after the Sunday morning service, when we all gathered for a potluck meal. Of course, we had *compañerismos* every time something special came up, such as the pastor's birthday or someone's graduation. We even sometimes had them for the occasion of "not having had one for a while."

All in all, these fellowships happened about once per month. On the Sunday before the fellowship, one of the ladies of the church would come around and hand each woman a little white slip of paper with what we were supposed to bring written on it. I always got assigned *"pan e hielo,"* which means bread and ice. (Yes, I could speak Spanish, but we all knew I couldn't cook Hispanic food like the other members could, so "bread and ice" was the safest thing to assign me.)

Then, the following Sunday, everyone would arrive with their covered dishes. We'd all store what we'd brought in the kitchen or the fellowship hall until after the service, when we'd gather and have a meal together, often with some entertainment included. It was a blast.

More recently, our family had fun at a fellowship hosted by my best friend's church. There was a great homemade potluck meal (yummmmm!), with plenty of tables set up for people to sit anywhere in the fellowship building. After the dinner, there were activities outside for the children, including a bounce house, a dunking booth, a Slip 'N Slide, and more bounce houses. Cotton candy and other refreshments were available. Our family had a superb time enjoying everything the event had to offer, and we were grateful for our friends' invitation.

Those kinds of get-togethers are great. In fact, church members ought to fellowship with one another on a regular basis. But meals and bounce houses and parties, or whatever other activity a church may plan, are not the only kinds of fellowship Christians need. If they are the only kinds that are taking place, we're missing part of the point of what fellowship is really all about.

True Christian fellowship involves more than just pursuing a particular activity together. The deepest kind of fellowship involves knowing and being intimately known by each other, standing with each other in times of trial, and encouraging or even rebuking each other when necessary. It's "iron sharpening iron." Two pieces of iron might lie side by side and get along fine, but unless they sharpen and are sharpened by each other, they'll never become what they were meant to be.

Let's look at how we sharpen each other and how this process helps us have abundant life. Specifically we will look at the following: knowing and being intimately known; regularly attending church; and demonstrating love for one another.

Iron Sharpening Iron

There are three ways in which iron can sharpen iron. The first way in which our fellowship sharpens us is through time spent together knowing each other and being known.

Knowing another person usually isn't all that scary. Being known, however, especially when you are intimately known, can be terrifying. That's because in order to be known, you have to make yourself open and vulnerable to others. When you do that, you run the risk of being hurt.

So why would God place us in communities with other believers and ask us to do something scary? Because together, we as believers form the Body of Christ; if parts of the Body are missing, we won't know what Christ's Body looks like, and we won't gain the understanding of Him that we could have otherwise.

> For just as the body is one and has many members, and all the members of the body, though many, are one body, so it is with Christ. For in one Spirit we were all baptized into one body—Jews or Greeks, slaves or free—and all were made to drink of one Spirit. For the body does not consist of one member but of many. If the foot should say, "Because I am not a hand, I do not belong to the body," that would not make it any less a part of the body. And if the ear should say, "Because I am not an eye, I do not belong to the body," that would not make it any less a part of the body. If the whole body were an eye, where would be the sense of hearing? If the whole body were an ear, where would be the sense of smell? (1 Cor. 12:12-17).

We're all part of the Body, and we all need one another. God has designed it this way so that we can all function together. In addition, we need one another in order to understand God better.

In Hebrews 10:24-25, we read, "And let us consider one another to provoke unto love and to good works: Not forsaking the assembling of ourselves together, as the manner of some is; but exhorting one another: and so much the more, as ye see the day approaching" (*KJV*).

We're also commanded, in James 5:16, "Therefore, confess your sins to one another and pray for one another, that you may be healed. The prayer of a righteous person has great power as it is working."

So we need one another to give us a fuller picture of the Body of Christ. We need one another to stir us up to love and good deeds. We need one another for encouragement; we need people to listen to us and pray for us when we've sinned. In order to receive these benefits of abundant life, we have to be willing to be vulnerable. Sure, sometimes we might get hurt. But the benefits far outweigh the potential risks.

We need fellowship for standing by one another in times of trial too. We're all going to face times of trial; during those times, we need the Body of Christ to uplift us and carry us along when we feel we just can't go any farther. We need them to strengthen and encourage us in our faith when it seems all is lost. We need them to remind us that life can be abundant and will be once again, even if right now life is tragically hard.

Second Corinthians 1:3-5 says:

Blessed be the God and Father of our Lord Jesus Christ, the Father of mercies and God of all comfort, who comforts us in all our affliction, so that we may be able to comfort those who are in any affliction, with the comfort with which we ourselves are comforted by God. For as we share abundantly in Christ's sufferings, so through Christ we share abundantly in comfort too.

In other words, we need other people to strengthen us when we stand and help us up when we fall. God has provided the Body of Christ for this, and we need them. What kind of life would we have if we had no one to help us when we were down or in trouble? It would be a lot more difficult to have abundant life, that's for sure.

The third reason we need fellowship is perhaps the most dicey. Oh, it's true, all right, but part of it requires something we're usually uncomfortable doing. That's because the third reason involves exhorting (encouraging to good works) and rebuking (correcting from sin). We love exhorting one another. Encouraging someone is relatively easy. It's fun, and people usually appreciate it. We can all think of times when someone encouraged us and made our day.

Rebuke, on the other hand, isn't any fun for anybody. Telling somebody he or she is wrong is never comfortable or pleasant. But it needs to be done, and we need to have it done for us in order to keep between the lines on the road to abundant life.

I remember a time when I had done something wrong and a friend had to talk to me about it. It wasn't a comfortable conversation for either of us, but my friend was right, and I knew it. While I didn't enjoy hearing what she had to say, I appreciated the fact that she cared enough about me to be willing to say something. What kind of friends are we if we never correct anyone's wrongdoing?

A well-known slogan, which is also a very valuable reminder, says, "Friends don't let friends drive drunk." Well, friends don't let friends continue in any kind of sin without saying something. It takes both bravery and love to confront someone in the right way—the godly way—so that they can come back to the "straight and narrow." But God says we need the Body of Christ for this, to help us keep on track toward abundant life.

Are you part of a group of people to whom you can be vulnerable, and who will be vulnerable to you? All of us have been in groups where the prayer requests were always on behalf of "my boss's friend's mom's aunt"; never would anyone say, "This request is for me. I'm struggling, and here's how." Certainly it's not wrong to pray for other people we know, but if we're unable to be transparent with one another, something is wrong. We need to be part

of a group where we can confess our sins and find not condem-
nation, but support and godly encouragement as we repent and
move forward. We also need to be that same resource for others.

The second way we sharpen each other is through regular
church attendance. It's not a matter of keeping score or checking
all the right boxes. It's a matter of being present. If we're not at
church (whether that means gathering in the church building or
meeting with a small group) on a regular basis, we're not going to
be of much use in building anyone up, and we won't be built up,
either. If we miss out on fellowship occasionally because of a valid
excuse, such as having a sick child or being out of town, that's one
thing. Everyone has times when run-of-the-mill things come up or
some emergency arises. But if we don't make Christian fellowship
a priority, Satan has plenty of influences at the ready to step into
our lives and fill the vacuum that should be filled by fellowship
with believers.

Third, and most important, we sharpen each other by demonstrating love for one another. This kind of love doesn't love merely
when we look our best on Sunday mornings or even just when we
act right. It loves under any circumstances, and forever. It's love
that results in action—that says, "I'll stand by you no matter what"
and "If you have a need, I'm there." It's always ready to encourage,
and it's even ready to rebuke when necessary. It seeks to help build
the loved one up into the image of Christ, whatever that takes.
It looks at what it can do for others, not at what others can do for
it. This kind of love is so amazingly incredible that it is the proof
that we follow Jesus (see John 13:34-35). It draws people to itself by
its very existence in a way that nothing else can. It's what frees us
to be vulnerable with one another and encourages us to keep going
when we don't think we can go on any longer. Most important, it's
what Jesus commanded us to do.

Are you part of a group whose members love one another deeply, see or talk with one another regularly, and are free to be vulnerable to one another? A group whose members serve together and

grow together, love and encourage one another, and stand by one another no matter what, no matter when?

If not, you need such a group. You need others to help you become all God wants you to be, and you need to help them too. If you don't know where to find this kind of fellowship, go before the Lord and ask Him to show you. He may direct you to an option you haven't thought about. He might show you some things you need to correct before you can experience—and offer—this kind of fellowship. He will do all of that, because He knows you need fellowship. After all, He made all of us, and He knows we need one another.

So, as moms, where do we find time for all this community? Some days, we barely have time to take a shower, much less cram one more thing into the schedule. Hopefully your church attendance will provide a good deal of what you need in this department. You're already going to be at church anyway, so if your church family provides the kind of fellowship we've been talking about, you won't need to find as much extra time in your schedule. If not, would it be possible to meet with a group of friends once a week or even once a month? Most of us can squeeze in one lunch date per month, if we really try. If we're so busy that we can't fit something like that in, maybe we're too busy. Maybe we should cut some other things out of our schedules instead of cutting out valuable community time.

It all depends on what's most important to us. I suggest that we prioritize the things God says are necessary to our abundant life. Prioritizing secondary things (or things even farther down on the list) will only clog our schedules and make us frazzled and stressed out so that we can't find time for what is truly important. Is there something you've been neglecting that really needs to be a part of your schedule? Like time in community, perhaps? What could you do to make sure community time gets put back in your schedule? Because after all, in order to have abundant life, you need others—and they need you.

Abundant Living Action Steps

1. Have you been neglecting fellowship with other believers? Make specific plans to reengage in that kind of fellowship.
2. What kind of fellowship could you offer to others? Make plans to do so.

For a more in-depth study of the topics of each chapter, see the Bible study at the end of this book.

Part 2

Abundant
Spiritual
Blessings

Beyond All We Ask or Imagine

*When something disappointing happened,
my mother would remind me not to let that become my focus.
There's still so much to be grateful for.*
KATHERINE HEIGL

We spent the last few chapters talking about different ways we as moms can experience abundant life. I hope that by this point, you're beginning to believe that your life *can* be abundant, even in the midst of the messiness.

Now let's talk about just how abundant it can be.

If you were to ask me about the greatest vacation I could imagine, I would tell you that it would definitely involve going to Europe. I'd visit as many countries as I could on that continent, staying in five-star hotels along the way. I'd have plenty of spending money (of course), and ample opportunity to use it. I'd stay on vacation for at least a month, checking out some of the sites I've always wanted to see but have only ever heard about.

What is the best vacation you could imagine? Would you go to Europe? Disney World? Would you take the kids? Would you leave them at home? Would you spend quiet days relaxing, or busy days seeing everything you could see? Maybe some of both?

I asked each of my four older children about the best gift they could imagine. Jessica wasn't sure what the best gift would be. But Lindsey chose "a thousand monkeys" (she collects monkeys), Kenny chose "a huge, gigantic Lego set," and Ellie aimed a little higher, choosing "all the video games in the world."

The fact is, however, that even these wonderful gifts would pale in comparison to what God can do for us. The apostle Paul tells us that God can do way beyond all we ask or imagine (see Eph. 3:20). I know I can imagine some pretty great things, and I'm sure you can too. Yet God can come up with things so great that they put even our biggest dreams to shame. He can give gifts that are far beyond Legos, video games, monkeys, or even a trip to Europe.

Not only can He come up with better *things*, but He can also bestow on us greater spiritual blessings than we ever thought to ask for—or He can bestow them in a greater way or to a greater degree than we ever imagined.

God is not a "halfway" God. He doesn't do things partially or just a little bit. He does what He does wholeheartedly, completely and perfectly, and that includes the way He gives us blessings that can't be seen or touched, such as spiritual blessings.

Remember Ephesians 1:3, where we read that God has blessed us with "every spiritual blessing"? It doesn't just say "a couple of" spiritual blessings. It doesn't even say "plenty of" spiritual blessings. It says "every" spiritual blessing.

Let's do the math: every spiritual blessing + abundantly more than we can ask or imagine = something truly incredible! It's unbelievable that God would choose to bless us sinners abundantly—to lavish upon us every spiritual blessing without holding some back as consequences for all our sins. Yet that's exactly what He's chosen to do. *Every* spiritual blessing, to an extent that's *abundantly more than we can ask or imagine*.

If this still sounds too incredible to believe, consider this: God doesn't start something and then not finish it. Numbers 23:19 tells us that He doesn't speak and then not act. He doesn't promise and then not fulfill. In other words, He doesn't say He's going to do something and then not do it. God keeps His word.

We also know from Hebrews 6:18 that it is impossible for God to lie. So He can't tell us something He never really meant in the first place. If He says it, it's true, because He can't lie. And if He says it, He will act upon it, because He's not like us puny human beings who sometimes fail to follow through on our promises.

Dare we really believe God? Dare we get our hopes up that these things really could be true for us?

They may be true for others, but not for me, you might think. *You don't know what I've done.*

Remember that God's promises aren't given only to those with perfect pasts. He's not faithful only to those who have a spotless record (which is nobody). He provides everything each of His children needs, no matter what. You can't deserve all His blessings, but you can still receive them, because you are His child—and as I said before, that will never change.

But it doesn't work that way in my life, you might be protesting. *My life isn't filled with abundant spiritual blessings.*

Oh, but it can be. God's spiritual blessings are available to each of His children any time they are needed. Your life can be filled with abundant spiritual blessings, even in the midst of the chaos of motherhood.

We've already said that the first blessing God bestows upon us is the privilege of getting to know Him—and He has granted us so many ways of getting to know Him that it's just incredible. We can pray. We can study our Bibles. We can attend worship services and participate in small groups. We can listen to worship music. We can fast. We can be frugal. We can give. We can _____ (fill in the blank with anything you can think of, and yes, you can probably come to know God through that).

We can know Him in the midst of the messiness. That's abundant life right there. In fact, the Bible confirms that for us in John 17:3: "Now this is eternal life: that they may know you, the only true God, and Jesus Christ, whom you have sent" (*NIV*).

True, this says that knowing God is "eternal" life, not "abundant" life. But we know from John 10:10 that Jesus promised to give us abundant life. So we can conclude that knowing Him means living abundantly, forever and ever.

God not only allows us to know Him, which is incredible enough in itself, but He also "sheds blessings abroad" into our hearts. In other words, He pours out things like love, peace, joy and strength into our lives. That's because to know Him is to know abundant life. In fact, Jesus said, "I am the way, and the truth, and the life" (John 14:6). So if we know Him, and He is all things—like love, peace, joy and strength— we will naturally have these things in our lives too. Make sense?

So why don't I feel very joyful? you may wonder. *I don't feel very peaceful, either. Some days I feel loving, some days not so much. And strength? Ha! I'm barely making it.*

Could it be that perhaps you don't know how to appropriate these spiritual blessings that God has made available to you? Could it be that you aren't fully aware of the extent to which He's woven them into your life?

Actually, that's true of all of us. None of us completely grasps the magnitude of the immense spiritual blessings God has poured out upon us and made available to us. But the extent to which we grasp them and understand where they come from and know where and how to look for them will determine the extent to which we find them in our lives.

In the next four chapters, we're going to look at four blessings that God produces abundantly in our lives: love, peace, joy and strength. We'll discuss what those look like for moms and where they come from. But before we go there, we need to talk about how God produces those things in our lives.

How God Produces Abundance in Our Lives

One way God does this is by producing what are commonly called the Fruit of the Spirit in our lives. These "fruit" are qualities that naturally result from the Holy Spirit's influence over us. It's safe to say that to the extent that the Holy Spirit influences a person, he or she will have the following spiritual qualities: "love, joy, peace, patience, kindness, goodness, faithfulness, gentleness and self-control" (Gal. 5:22-23, *NIV*).

These are not qualities we can simply determine to have within ourselves and muster up on our own. Sure, we can determine to be patient, for example, and we may be patient outwardly, but without the Holy Spirit's influence, we will not feel peaceful inwardly. Or we can try to be good, but the Bible tells us that even our best efforts aren't any better than filthy rags (see Isa. 64:6). Without the Holy Spirit guiding our lives, we won't be truly good.

We may be able to fool people for a while, but we won't fool God. He is well aware of who is submitting herself to His influence and who is striking out on her own and doing her own thing. He knows who realizes that she needs the Holy Spirit's help to produce anything good in her because she can't do it on her own.

You and I need the Holy Spirit in our lives if we are to have the abundant spiritual blessings we mentioned earlier. Fortunately, if we have accepted Christ's sacrifice for us and asked Him to be Lord of our lives, He has sent the promised Holy Spirit to dwell within us and do God's work of conforming our lives to His. So if you're a Christian, you have the Holy Spirit within you.

But it's possible to grieve the Holy Spirit. Paul warns, "And do not grieve the Holy Spirit of God, with whom you were sealed for the day of redemption" (Eph. 4:30, *NIV*).

What does it mean to grieve the Holy Spirit? It means to do things that do not please Him. Things that make Him sad. Things He knows are sin—or at the very least aren't good for us and won't build us up into the women He wants us to be.

We grieve Him when we don't know Him. We also grieve Him when we don't listen to His voice. Jesus said that the Holy Spirit would guide us into all truth (see John 16:13). One thing we know is true is that Christ loves us deeply and passionately. The Holy Spirit keeps reminding us of this, but sometimes we don't believe Him. Either that, or we just kind of ignore His whispers of truth because we don't "get" how much He loves us.

I believe that this grieves the Holy Spirit too. He's whispering to us (or, sometimes, shouting to us) about how much God loves us, but we don't listen. We continue to believe that God doesn't really love us all that much.

Maybe it's because we grew up in environments where we were unloved. Maybe we've had bad experiences in the past where people who were supposed to love us have betrayed us. Whatever the reason, we no longer believe we're all that lovable.

My friend, if this describes you, it's time to start believing what God says is true and not what your thoughts or emotions tell you is true. You can make a decision of your will to believe that God loves you and to start acting like it, even if it doesn't really "feel" true at this point.

The devil doesn't want it to feel true, because he knows that most of us will proceed based on our feelings rather than on our knowledge of the truth. He's thrilled about this, because feelings are so easy to manipulate and deceive. Don't let him do it any longer! You know better, even if you don't feel like you do. Determine that you will listen to the Holy Spirit's voice instead of the voices of your mother, your husband, your friend, Satan, and anyone else who is trying to tell you otherwise.

If this is a struggle for you, I understand. I've been there. But I've also come out the other side of it now, and that's how I know that God's love is real. I've experienced it. If you need someone to walk alongside you as you work on believing what God says instead of what you feel, contact me through the information found in the back of this book. I'll walk with you. And God will too.

The second thing the Holy Spirit keeps trying to tell us that we often misunderstand is that abundant life is to be found in God alone, not anyplace else. Too often we've convinced ourselves—or allowed others to convince us—that abundant life can only be found in having perfect circumstances, making enough money, or getting that job we want. But as we've already seen, abundant life consists in knowing God.

The Holy Spirit keeps trying to tell us this, but instead of listening, we pursue anything and everything else we think will help us fill up that emptiness inside. The problem is, nothing else is ever going to satisfy us. Only in knowing God can truly abundant life be found, and we grieve the Holy Spirit when our actions show that we don't believe Him when He tells us that.

Precious mom, the God who is and does abundantly more than we can ask or imagine longs for you to believe Him when He tries to remind you that He loves you and that abundant life can only be found in His love. If we don't get these two basics down, it will be next to impossible for God to shed other things into our lives—like love, peace, joy and strength.

Will you believe the Holy Spirit, precious mom? If you will, you make room for blessings that are abundantly more than you can ask or imagine. So if you can imagine some pretty great things, and God can do abundantly more than that, well . . . you are in for an incredible treat.

Now let's look at the first of these blessings: love.

Abundant Living Action Steps

1. Do you believe that God really loves you? I mean, do you really *believe* it? Declare to God right now that you do, and ask Him to help you live as though it's true—because it is!

2. Is there anything you're asking God for that only He can do? If not, why not? Go before Him in prayer and ask Him to help you dream bigger.

For a more in-depth study of the topics of each chapter, see the Bible study at the end of this book.

Abundant Love

The one thing I never questioned about my mother
was whether she loved me.
LORNA LUFT

While searching the Internet for quotations about love, I came across some pretty interesting ones:

- "You're the ketchup to my fries."
- "You can't buy love, because when it's real, it's priceless."
- "Love is laughing."
- "Distance is just a test to see how far love can travel."
- "You are the icing on my cupcake."
- "You never fall in love the same way twice."

There were thousands more. Some were serious; some were funny. The few sampled here give you an idea of how varied the ideas are out there about what love is.

When I was younger, my idea of what love was was different from what I now know it to be. From everything I could tell from books and movies, love was this overwhelming feeling that lasted intensely forever. At least, that's how it seemed to be portrayed in popular media.

When I got married, however, I discovered that love takes work. Good relationships have to be worked on. You can't just sit back and enjoy them without ever doing things to maintain them. I learned that for marriages to work, both partners have to be willing to put time and effort into the relationship. Fortunately, both my husband and I have been willing to invest in ours, and we're still married, 18 years later.

I have also learned during the past 18 years that love isn't always warm, fluffy feelings. Sometimes the feelings will be intense; sometimes they won't. Just because they're not intense all the time doesn't mean you don't love that person anymore.

So I learned a lot about love from my marriage, and I'm still learning. But when I became a mom, I began to learn even more about love. A whole new kind of love opened to me—a kind I had never experienced before, and which I never would have experienced had I not become a mom.

Let's talk about three aspects of this incredible love God has poured into our lives: love for our children, love from our children, and love for others who love our children.

Love for Our Children

We touched on this earlier when we talked about being better able to understand God's love for us because of the love we have for our children. But let's look a little deeper at this love.

Before I had children, I never knew how much love my heart was capable of. Even now, I am still learning as I grow as a parent and my love for my children deepens. But now I know—and you know—this love that defies complete expression in words.

It is a love that does three things for us: teaches us how to love someone more than we love ourselves; causes us to seek our children's good even above our own; and changes us forever, in a wonderful way.

Loving someone more than we love ourselves can be hard. No, it *is* hard. We human beings are born selfish, and it's hard to put others first. That's one reason the love we have for our children is one of God's greatest gifts to us. Not just because it feels good—great!—to love someone like that, but because it gets us to look beyond ourselves and put our focus on others.

Without such a powerful force as love for our children, most of us would still be stuck loving ourselves more than we love anyone else on earth. But when we had children, something inside *compelled* us to learn to love them more than we love ourselves. In fact, as I shared earlier, this love can turn even nonviolent women into moms who would kill to protect their babies if that became necessary. You know what I mean. It's a love that's so deep it says we would do *whatever it takes* to protect our loved ones—in this case, our children.

This incredible love for our children not only feels wonderful and teaches us to love someone else more than we love ourselves, but it also gives us a glimpse into how madly, passionately God is in love with us. Because if we, being human, can love like this, how much more passionately can God love His children?!

What an incredible gift!

The second aspect of love that we as mothers can understand in a way we wouldn't otherwise is love *from* our children.

I remember a time when Kenny was about four years old. Phil and I and our kids (at that time, we only had four) were all at Phil's parents' home for the weekend. That Sunday, we attended Sunday School with his parents. After that, it was time for church.

That's where the problems started. There was some uncertainty as to whether there would be children's church or whether the kids might have to sit in the service with us. First, Kenny (who at the time was diagnosable with Asperger's and related special needs) was told that there would be children's church. Then he was told that there wouldn't. Then we started down the hall to where children's church was supposed to be, having been told that there was children's church after all. Then we found out (definitively, this time) that no, there was no children's church.

Poor Kenny began to get upset by all the changes in what he expected. He was overwhelmed by what was going on, and he began to cry and tremble. I knew at that point that what he really needed was a place where he could calm down, so Phil's mom and I took Kenny and then-baby Jessica back to the house. While Phil's mom prepared lunch, I nursed Jessica in the den as Kenny played nearby with a train set.

It was a peaceful moment. Jessica nursed easily, and Kenny had calmed down and was having a good (if serious) time playing with the trains. We sat together in companionable silence until Kenny stopped playing with his trains and just sat there.

Not looking up at me, he said, "You make a good mom." He paused, then added, "A good friend." Then he got up, came over to me, and, still without looking at me, laid his head in my lap.

I stroked his hair. After a few seconds, he returned to playing with his trains, and that was that. Or at least it was as far as he was concerned. I have remembered it ever since and will remember it until the day I die.

Why? Because it was a precious, sweet moment in which Kenny showed me just how much he loved and appreciated me.

At four years old, and with his special needs, he didn't know how to say, "Mommy, thanks for understanding my needs and doing something about them. Thanks for taking me home where I could be comfortable. Thanks for understanding. I really appreciate it."

But the words he did use communicated the same thing.

I'm sure you too can think of things your children have done to show you they love you. Things that may not have seemed like a big deal at the time—or to them—but which you remember to this day. Those super-special moments don't happen every day. They may not even happen every week. But they do happen, and when they do, they touch something so deep in our hearts that we never forget.

Our children show us that they love us in everyday, ordinary moments too. Maybe they give us a picture they drew, on which they carefully printed "To Mommy." Maybe they got half the letters backward, but it doesn't matter. We treasure that artwork—delivered with a smile on our child's face—as if it were a Rembrandt.

Why? Because it's great art? No, because it came from a heart of pure love.

Or maybe they come give us a hug before running off to play, or they wrap their arms tightly around us as we tuck them in bed. Those are moments of pure love too.

Let me share with you some other moments that we all experience from time to time, which we may never have thought of as expressions of our children's love for us:

- When our child cleans something we didn't ask her to clean, just to surprise us (even if it's not done very well).
- When our child obeys without arguing.
- When she picks us a flower.
- When he brings us a roly-poly.
- Spontaneous I-love-yous.
- When our child holds our hand unexpectedly.
- When she asks our opinion.
- When he shows concern for us when we're not feeling well.

You see? If we include all these ordinary things, our children are constantly telling us that they love us. And guess what? God is the one who made our children in such a way that they delight to do these things for us. I believe He did so not only because He wanted to knit our hearts together with theirs, but also because He wanted us to know that He cares about our feeling loved. You see, God didn't have to make our children desire to shower us with love, yet He did. He wants us to feel loved, and He wants us to know that He cares about our being able to feel that way.

There is a third aspect to this mother-love, in addition to love for our children and love from our children, and that is love for others who love our children.

My four older children recently spent the week with my in-laws in order to attend Vacation Bible School at my in-laws' church. Actually, the three oldest attended VBS, while Jessica got to stay home and have Grandma all to herself for such activities as baking her favorite kind of cookies. All four kids had a blast, and I think

Grandma and Pampa did too (though I'm sure they're glad that quiet has returned to their house).

I feel incredibly blessed that my kids have grandparents they can go and stay with—grandparents who will love on them, play with them, and, best of all, teach them that loving and following Jesus is important. Just as my kids love their grandparents, I love them like crazy too.

One of the reasons I love them so much is that they love my children very much. It shows in everything they do—from inviting the kids to their house, to giving birthday and Christmas gifts, to spending time with them, to baking cookies, to playing video games with them, to taking them out for special treats. When I see someone loving on my children like that, I love that person even more.

If you are blessed to have loving grandparents in your children's lives, or other loving adults your children spend time with, you know exactly what I'm talking about. When someone loves our children and treats them lovingly, we naturally respond with love for that person. That's the third aspect of this mother-love that God has poured into our hearts.

But there's one more point to consider about this kind of love, and that is that while we understand loving another person because he or she loves our children, we don't always think about how God feels about us when we love His children. In other words, you know that love you have for those who love your kids? God has that same love for you when you love not only His Son, Jesus, but also His other children.

Have you ever thought about it that way? That part of God's love for you is because you love His children? Just like we do as moms, so too God so closely identifies with His children that He feels loved when we love His children—and not just His Son, Jesus, but His other children too (including both little children, as well as anyone of any age who knows Jesus and is therefore His child). When you show love to those with whom God identifies, His heart is stirred toward you.

In fact, in some of Jesus' last moments of teaching on this earth, He emphasized to His disciples how important it is for us to love one another. He told them, "A new command I give you: Love one another. As I have loved you, so you must love one another" (John 13:34, *NIV*). Part of the reason for this command is what He goes on to say in verse 36—that everyone will know we are His disciples if we love one another. But another part of the reason for His command must surely be that He wants His children to be loved.

Remember Matthew 25:40? "Whatever you did for one of the least of these brothers of mine, you did for me" (*NIV*). Jesus so closely identifies with people considered "the least of these" (including children) that He takes personally what is done to them. So when you love His children, you love Him—and He loves you for it.

Through motherhood, then, we come to know a very special kind of love—a love for our kids, from our kids, and for those others who love our kids. And through this love, we get further glimpses of God's abundant love for us.

Abundant Living Action Steps

1. What are some things you can purposely do to show love to each person in your family? Make a list.
2. Now make specific plans to show love to each person in your family.

> For a more in-depth study of the topics of each chapter,
> see the Bible study at the end of this book.

Abundant Peace

Mother's love is peace. It need not be acquired,
it need not be deserved.
ERICH FROMM

How would you complete the following sentence: "There is peace in our home when . . ."?

    a. the kids are asleep
    b. the kids are gone
    c. no one is home
    d. everyone is well-rested
    e. there is laughter
    f. nobody's fighting
    g. the house is clean
    h. Mommy and Daddy aren't stressed
    i. we do things together
    j. we pray together

All of these were answers given to a recent Facebook poll I took on the subject. *A* and *B* seemed to be the most popular answers.

As a mom of five children, believe me, I understand those two answers. On some days, they would be my top choices too!

But fortunately, God has made it possible for us as moms to be at peace all the time, not just when the kids aren't bothering us. Yes, you read that right. *All* the time.

How in the world is that *supposed to happen?* you might wonder, and with good reason. *How can I be at peace when my house is a wreck, my kids are fighting, and we just got the electric bill?*

Good question. In fact, great question. That's what this chapter is about: how to be at peace all the time, not just when circumstances are perfect. Because if we wait until circumstances are perfect, we'll be waiting a long time.

There is indeed a certain kind of peace that comes when everything's going right. (I love those times. Don't you?) There's nothing wrong with enjoying that kind of peace. In fact, there's everything right about enjoying it and thanking God for it.

But that's not what we're talking about here. It's not hard for us to feel at peace during those times. It's easy. When we need help is when circumstances are very much "not perfect." That's when being at peace is hard.

Let's make it clear what kind of peace we're talking about. The best kind of peace comes not from circumstances, but from a sense of well-being deep within our souls. Check out Jesus' promise: "Peace I leave with you; my peace I give you. I do not give to you as the world gives. Do not let your hearts be troubled and do not be afraid" (John 14:27, *NIV*).

Jesus was talking to His disciples shortly before His arrest and crucifixion. He was talking to people who were about to go through times when circumstances were very much "not okay." Yet He told them that peace was possible, even in the midst of what they were about to endure.

Let's look at Jesus' words more closely so that we can see how this peace that goes beyond our understanding (see Phil. 4:7) looks in the life of a mom.

"Peace I Leave with You"

Here it is again: Jesus' promise of peace. He wasn't saying that the disciples might have peace, or that perhaps they could manufacture some if they tried hard enough and were really lucky. He was saying, "Here it is. I give you peace. It's here."

Granted, the disciples probably didn't feel too peaceful in the days that followed. But again, Jesus *promised* that they would have peace and told them that He had made it available to them.

They may not have known how to appropriate it, just as you and I sometimes don't know how to appropriate God's peace either. We'll talk about "how" later in this chapter. Just notice first that peace *is* available. That's a promise.

"My Peace I Give You"

Jesus said this because He wanted to make it clear exactly what kind of peace He was offering. He was offering His disciples *His* peace—the peace that both resides in Him and emanates from Him. This kind of peace is a soul-deep peace, such that our souls can be at rest even in the midst of undesirable circumstances. It's a peace that says, like the old hymn, that "it is well with my soul" no matter what might be true around us.

The man who wrote that hymn, Philip Bliss, knew the kind of peace Jesus was talking about. He and his family had planned on making a trip from America to France on an ocean liner together, but at the last minute, Philip had to stay behind to deal with business concerns arising from the Great Chicago Fire. His wife and four daughters sailed without him.

During the voyage, their ship collided with another vessel and sank. All four of his daughters drowned. His wife, Anna, sent him a telegram saying only, "Saved alone."

Yet Philip later penned the words to the great hymn "It Is Well with My Soul," some of which include:

When peace, like a river, attendeth my way,
When sorrows like sea billows roll,

Whatever my lot, Thou hast taught me to say,
"It is well. It is well with my soul."

In other words, despite the horrific circumstance of losing his four precious daughters, Philip's soul was able to be at rest because of the peace that Jesus gives.

This peace is not based on circumstances. It's based on the knowledge that one is saved and loved—madly and passionately—by God, and that no matter what else may be true, that fact is so overwhelmingly joyous that it is still well with our souls even when sorrows roll upon us.

This is a peace that the world cannot give, because the world does not know how to be at peace unless circumstances are perfect. This is a peace that only Jesus can give. Don't forget that He promised to give it, and He cannot lie or change His mind. This peace is available to any mom, anywhere, if she will only accept it from Jesus.

"I Do Not Give to You as the World Gives"

Not only does Jesus give a different kind of peace than the world can possibly offer, but He also gives it in a way that the world cannot and does not give.

The world offers peace as a greeting. Jesus offers a lasting peace that goes far deeper than mere good wishes.

The world offers peace when you've done everything "right." Jesus offers peace even when you've done something wrong, if you will repent of your wrong doing and seek His forgiveness.

The world offers peace by convincing us that we can have perfect circumstances. Jesus offers peace despite our not having perfect circumstances, which He knows we will rarely (if ever) have.

The world offers peace that it will turn around and take away in a heartbeat. Jesus offers peace that He will never take away.

So He does not give to us as the world gives. The peace He offers is far better, far deeper and far longer-lasting.

"Do Not Let Your Hearts Be Troubled and Do Not Be Afraid"

We do have a part to play in all this, and in this portion of His remarks, Jesus explains what that part is. We have to make the choice not to allow ourselves to remain troubled or afraid.

Jesus isn't saying that we can always choose our circumstances. He is saying that whatever circumstances we find ourselves in, we can choose to accept His peace and not let our minds and hearts dwell upon the what-ifs and the how-terribles.

When we're going through a difficult time in life, it's natural for our circumstances to come into our minds and threaten to upset us. But we have the choice either to become upset and turn those circumstances over and over in our minds, becoming more and more fretful, or to say, "whatever my lot, Thou hast taught me to say it is well with my soul."

How can we choose to say that it is well with our souls in the midst of difficult circumstances? The same way Philip Bliss chose to say it. He recognized that despite the agonizing grief he felt, his soul was still taken care of and still cared for. He chose Christ's peace. I'm sure he must still have cried and grieved at times, probably for the rest of his life. But each time, he chose to come back to what he knew to be true—that no matter what happened to him, he was okay, because Jesus had taken care of his soul.

That, my friends, is what lasting peace—peace that can't be shaken no matter the circumstances—is all about.

Bringing Peace to Our Family

Not only does Christ bring peace to our hearts, but He also gives us the ability to bring peace to our families. Maybe not perfect peace, as He can give, but peace nonetheless that at least lasts for a time. There are two primary ways we can do this: by bringing peace to our family members and by bringing peace to our surroundings, including our schedule.

Bringing Peace to Family Members

Sometimes, the bickering between siblings seems to last all day. If you're like me, it's tempting just to send everyone to his or her own room, where they have no one to talk to, so that the quarreling will stop—and sometimes I do that. That's one of the ways we can force the fighting to stop—by separating the siblings who are engaging in it.

Another way to bring peace between siblings is a little bit more lighthearted. Lisa Whelchel explains this strategy in her book *Creative Correction*. The idea is that when kids have been bickering, they need to be reminded that when it comes down to it, they really do love each other. So they are made to sit or stand facing each other. Then the first child has to say, "I love you," and sound like he or she means it. The second child has to respond, equally sincerely, "I love you." Then they have to alternate saying it until each child has said it five times. So far, each time we've done this in my family, the bickerers have wound up laughing so hard they can barely get the words out the last couple times, and the bickering has been resolved.

The means you use to bring peace between siblings is up to you. Be creative! You know what kinds of things will work for your family. If you're stuck for ideas (as we all are sometimes), check out a book such as Lisa's. She makes lots of great suggestions. Or ask your friends what they do. Then, whatever method you choose, enjoy the fact that you've been able to help bring peace to your family, at least for a little while.

Of course, bringing about truces between siblings is helpful, but it's not the most valuable way you can bring peace to your family. The most valuable way is to introduce your children to peace with God. Teach them about God. Tell them how wonderful He is and how much He loves them. Tell them what Jesus did on their behalf. Invite them to accept His gift. Perhaps your children will accept Christ, and you will have had a part in bringing to them the greatest peace the world has ever known: peace between God and man.

You can also bring peace to your family by doing your best to get along with your husband. I understand that there are some times when he will mistreat you or sin against you. I'm not suggesting that your husband is always perfect. But many times, we are far more demanding of our husbands than we are of ourselves. We want our husbands to show us completely perfect love, reactions and attitudes, and if they don't (or if they do something else we think is wrong), we nag them about it.

What difference might it make in your home if you were to start with yourself in the effort to get along better with your husband? You can't change him, but you can change your reactions to him, and you can change the way you treat him. Not only will this bring peace between you and your husband, but it will also bring more peace among your children.

One time, my husband and I were arguing. We weren't raising our voices or calling each other names, but we were arguing nonetheless. After we had ended our argument and gone our separate ways, Ellie (then about six years old) said, "I hate it when you guys argue. It just makes me feel all bad inside."

Poor thing. Kids shouldn't have to listen to parents argue. Disagree in loving, respectful ways, fine. But argue? No.

What can *you* do to help bring peace to your children by getting along better with your husband? Could you stop arguing with him? Could you accept his answers or viewpoint more often than you do? Could you simply let him be right when it's merely a matter of opinion and not of fact?

Think about it. None of us is perfect, so all of us have something we could do to be easier to get along with. Are you willing to do your part to bring this kind of abundance into your home? For your husband's sake, your children's sake, and even your own sake?

Bringing Peace to Our Schedules
This one can be a little challenging at times. I'm talking about bringing peace both to our homes and to our schedules.

Let's look at schedules first. For example, tomorrow is a difficult day for me, schedule-wise. My husband and I have to take the kids to childcare at the Y while we go work out there in the morning. Then, in the early afternoon, I have to take all the kids but Jessica to a doctor's appointment. Phil has to take Jessica to a different doctor. Later, I have to take Lindsey and all her siblings but Jessica (who will still be with Phil) to Lindsey's gymnastics class. It will be challenging to have Timmy with me for all those events and try to keep him entertained. He's a good little traveler, but he doesn't always like being schlepped around everywhere and expected to remain in his stroller.

We'll just have to see how it goes tomorrow, because there's not much I can do about the schedule at this point. But often, there are things I can do to make our schedule easier on us.

I'm a person who finds it easy to say no—when I want to, anyway. When I want to say yes to something, I tend to cram it into our schedule and make a way for it to happen, never mind how busy our lives get. I very much have to guard myself against this tendency. There have been times when I have had to say no to certain activities I would have enjoyed participating in because of what they would do to our schedule. There have been other times when I had to say no to activities that would benefit one of the children, again because of what it would have done to the schedule for the rest of us.

Perhaps you need to do that too—to say no to some of the things you would like to be able to say yes to in order to keep your schedule from driving you crazy. I have a friend who's great at this. For example, yesterday my kids and I were at a play date at her house. My daughter asked me if Sarah's daughter could come home with us after the play date, and I told her it was okay with me if it was okay with Sarah. When my daughter asked Sarah, however, Sarah said kindly, "No, I'm sorry. She can't." She was gracious about her response, but she was also firm. Sarah wanted to keep her schedule free that evening, and having to come pick up her child 25 minutes away at my house would have interfered with that. I completely understood that, and I admired her ability to say a firm no, and to say it in such a gracious way.

Perhaps your difficulty is not in saying no to things you want to do, but in saying no to things you don't want to do. Some of us have trouble saying no any time we're asked to do anything. Therefore, we wind up with a schedule that's jam-packed with things that aren't really beneficial to us or to our families, and then we resent it. How much more abundant would our lives be if we chose to say no to the things that wouldn't be good for us, as Sarah did?

Bringing Peace to Our Surroundings

Another way God has given us the ability to bring abundance into our lives and the lives of those around us is by bringing peace to our surroundings. I mention this one carefully and with all due sensitivity, because believe me, Martha Stewart does not live at my house. I don't make my own potpourri, and I've never folded a napkin into the shape of a swan. But wherever we fall on the domesticity spectrum, we can all maintain a certain level of cleanliness that helps bring peace to our homes.

Around my house, many times, the last thing to get done is the cleaning. It seems like everything else takes priority—the tyranny of the urgent. I understand that. I really do. But I have been learning lately that keeping the house clean will actually bring me more peace than leaving it dirty does. Let me suggest just a few ways this might be possible for you without adding more burdens to your already full day.

First, do you require the children to clean up their messes at least once a day? Perhaps before bedtime? Unless children are not old enough to have the physical ability to clean up after themselves, and/or do not have the linguistic ability to understand what you say, they can help keep the house clean. I have found that 10 minutes spent having the children clean up at night does wonders in terms of leaving the house in a state I can at least tolerate the next morning. Of course, it's also better if I have the kids clean up for

5 or 10 minutes at various times during the day as well. For example, I just offered my children the opportunity to earn a little media time by doing some extra cleaning, and they jumped at the chance. Let them earn some privileges. If they love media time, or riding-their-bikes time, or some other kind of time, let them earn it by doing extra chores. Not everything has to be handed to your kids free of charge.

Second, do you periodically go through your house and get rid of things you don't need? Maybe you can have a garage sale or simply donate toys to your favorite charity. Let your kids help you select what to donate (unless, as is the case with mine, every toy would immediately become their favorite and they would be unable to give anything away).

Third, do you periodically make yourself spend 5 to 10 minutes cleaning up? I'll bet if you were willing to give up some of your Facebook time (at least, that's what it is for me), you could make good progress in keeping your house clean. Many times we think we don't have time, but we really do, if we would only prioritize cleaning.

Let me say again, for the record, that your house doesn't have to be perfect. It does not need to look like it is ready for a real estate showing all the time (unless, of course, you really are trying to sell it). But a few minutes spent cleaning here and there will not only give you a sense of accomplishment, but it will also help bring peace to your home by keeping your stuff under control.

Peace in our hearts. Peace to those under our roof. Peace to our surroundings. God has made all of these abundantly possible; thanks be to Him.

Abundant Living Action Steps

1. In what ways are you not at peace right now? Spend some time laying these before God and asking for His peace.
2. What are some ways in which you could bring peace into your home or to your family members? Which of these ways will you put into practice first?

For a more in-depth study of the topics of each chapter, see the Bible study at the end of this book.

Abundant Joy

Joy is what happens to us when we allow ourselves
to recognize how good things really are.
MARIANNE WILLIAMSON

Watching your youngest daughter giggle as she holds a lizard in her hands.

When your child finds joy in you equal to the joy you have in him.

Carefully built Lego creations.

Seeing your child discover her passion.

Watching your children become the people God made them to be.

All of these things (the results of another Facebook poll) bring joy to our hearts as mothers. And there are many more—millions or billions, even. That's because, as moms, our lives can be so overflowing with joy that we feel incapable of containing it all.

Do we realize it? Not always. It's easy to see the drudgery and unpleasant aspects of motherhood. It's sometimes harder to focus on the positive aspects. Oh, sure, it's easy when everything is going right. But when that's not the case, we tend to focus on what's going wrong rather than on all the joy that's right there in front of us (which we're missing out on).

But you see, in addition to being a God of love and peace, God is also a God of joy. In fact, "joy" was His idea. Where else do you think it came from, if not from the mind of God? We frail, imperfect human beings would have no way of inventing a concept that so completely boggles the mind and permeates our daily lives. We'd have no idea of the millions of ways joy could be infused into our lives. We couldn't orchestrate as much joy for ourselves as God orchestrates for us.

There are two kinds of joy that God pours into our lives: joy that comes from circumstances, and joy that's soul-deep, just as peace can be, no matter the circumstances.

Two Kinds of Joy

We can, and should, find joy in the blessings God pours into our lives. We should delight when things happen that are fun or pleasing; this is what God means for us to do. He pours out His blessings so that we can enjoy (there's that word—"joy") them, not just brush them off as no big deal. He wants us to find pleasure in all the things He does for us. So it's not wrong to do so. It's absolutely right—as long as we realize that there's another kind of joy that's present even when the happy, "I just love the way this is going!" kind of joy isn't.

Let's start by looking at circumstantial joy.

Circumstantial Joy

This is the kind of joy we feel when our child gets dressed without complaining, when he brings us a picture, or when she cleans her room without arguing about it. In other words, when something fun or pleasant happens.

God knows we need encouragement as moms. (In fact, for a whole book about that very topic, see my previous book, *Well Done, Good and Faithful Mommy*.) He's well aware that sometimes things can go badly and be discouraging. So He fashioned our little people into creatures who love to bring joy into our lives and do so just by their very nature.

That's why our children do things like draw pictures for us, bring us interesting things they found, or do nice things for us. They're made to want to show us their love so that we have cause for joy. Don't you experience a little bit of joy when your child does something like that? Of course you do. So do I. And God has made these moments in our lives abundant so that we can experience abundant joy and an abundant life. Isn't that great and gracious of Him?

Deeper Joy
But there's an even deeper joy we feel at times—a joy so deep words can't express it. This joy comes to us at times such as when we stand in the doorway to our child's room and watch him sleep, or when we cuddle together on the couch and all seems right with the world. Yes, there is circumstantial joy at those times too. But the circumstance touches a deeper kind of joy within us that it's hard to truly understand until we're a parent. Joy that we probably didn't experience before we became moms. But joy that now over-flows into every aspect of our being.

Even when it's unobtrusive, it's there, needing only a reminder to allow us to tap into it. God has provided us this kind of joy so that even when circumstances aren't to our liking, we have some-thing to fall back on. We never have to go without joy in our spirits, because this kind of joy always remains with us, even when circum-stantial joy is lacking.

But these two are not the only kinds of joy God pours into our lives. He also overwhelms us with other reasons for joy.

Reasons for Joy
Other Than Our Children

In addition to our children, there are four other reasons for joy with which God has filled our lives. Let's look at each one of these.

The first is the joy of knowing Him. We've said before that knowing Him brings abundant life. That means joy! It's simply not possible to know God in a genuine way yet have a spirit that is less than joyful on a consistent basis. Or put another way, to the extent that we know God, our spirits will be joyful.

This doesn't mean that you have to go around smiling all the time, like some kind of Pollyanna. But it does mean that when you truly know God, you will be a joyful person. Joy will characterize you. People will know you as joyful. Granted, there will be times when you have a bad day or find yourself in a bad mood. But those times will not be typical of you. Instead, you will typically be joyful.

I'm sure you can think of people who are fun to be around because they're so joyful. True, some of these people may not be Christians and may just tend toward happiness as part of their personality. That's possible. But because true joy is to be found in God, if you know Him, you will generally be joyful. Make sense? How could you know such a wonderful Person intimately and yet not be joyful? You can't. It's just not possible. Not on a regular basis, anyway.

Many, many Bible verses talk about being joyful in the Lord. Here are just a few of them:

I will rejoice in the LORD; I will take joy in the God of my salvation (Hab. 3:18).

Then shall the trees of the forest sing for joy before the LORD, for he comes to judge the earth (1 Chron. 16:33). (If the trees will sing at the Lord's presence, don't you think we would too?)

And now my head shall be lifted up above my enemies all around me, and I will offer in his tent sacrifices with shouts of joy; I will sing and make melody to the LORD (Ps. 27:6).

Joy in the Lord. Joy in His presence. Joy in knowing Him. The Lord has made it possible for us to have this abundant joy all the time, because He will never leave us or forsake us (see Heb. 13:5).

The second reason for joy other than our children is our family and/or friends. Before we discuss this reason, let me say that I understand that sometimes family relationships are difficult. That's why I wrote "and/or." Some of your family may not be a joy to you. I know that's a possibility. But perhaps there are some in your family, or maybe close friends, who bring joy to your heart. So let's go ahead and talk about this reason for joy.

Ecclesiastes 4:12 tells us that a rope made out of three strands can't be easily broken. It's true. Take a three-strand rope and try to snap it or even pull it in half. I'm willing to bet that you won't be able to do it. In this metaphor, the three strands represent you, God, and a family member or friend who stands with you. It's a joyful thing to have people who will stand with you no matter what, so that when troubles come, you can't be snapped in half. You can rest in the security of knowing that someone is there for you—not just God (as if He weren't enough), but someone here on earth as well. This is a great and significant cause for joy.

Having loving family members or friends in your life is also a cause for joy because of the sheer pleasure you get from being in their company. If there's someone in whose company you can be, and be yourself, and laugh and have fun together—or cry together when necessary—that person is a treasure indeed, and a cause for joy.

Have you ever thought about it that way? Have you thought about how God is pouring joy into your life by allowing you to have relationships with people whom you love and who love you? How having them in your life is a joy, and spending time in their presence is a joy? It's true—and it's one of the most special ways God has granted us joy.

Another cause for joy is the many blessings He has given us. We've said before that we are supposed to enjoy them, and indeed we are. He means for them to be enjoyed and delighted in. That's one of the reasons He gave them to us—to give us something to be joyful about. True, our deepest joy doesn't come from circumstances, but when circumstances *are* to our liking, we should rejoice and be joyful about that.

What are some of the possessions you have that you enjoy? Would you include your house, your car, a piano, a smartphone, an iPad (or any other i-device), a computer, nice clothes, a great set of cookware? Have you ever thought that one of the reasons God allowed these things to come into your life was for your joy? Thanks be to God for all the pleasing things He gives us that we don't deserve and that He doesn't have to give!

A fourth reason for joy apart from our children is getting to do things we like to do. We may not get to do what we want to do every single time we identify something we want, but most of us get at least occasional opportunities to do things we like to do—things like going out with friends, reading a book, sitting on the front porch drinking coffee, making a favorite meal, or enjoying a dessert.

These, too, are things God places into our lives for our enjoyment. Things He gave *you* for *your* enjoyment. Make it personal. What things has God allowed you to do that bring you pleasure and joy? Make a list. (Writing things down helps cement them in our minds.) Go over each item on the list and thank God for it, acknowledging the joy you feel because of it.

You see how God has poured joy into your life in ways you might not even have thought of before? All these things are for your enjoyment.

All these things, together with the soul-deep joy He has promised you, are to give you abundant life.

There's one final thought I want to share in this chapter. First, go back and re-read the quotation from Marianne Williamson at the beginning. Better yet, I'll reproduce it for you here: "Joy is what happens to us when we allow ourselves to recognize how good things really are."

Let's talk for just a minute about our tendency to be negative. There are some people who have a tendency to find the good things in life. These people look on the bright side and see the positive in any situation. Other people tend to focus almost exclusively on the negative. They can see the bad even in a positive situation.

Most of us are somewhere in the middle. We have our good days, and we have our bad days. Sometimes we look on the bright side of things; sometimes, not so much.

But take a moment to consider how often you might be a negative person. Does being negative characterize you? Is it more than just an occasional thing with you? If you're not sure, ask someone you trust to be honest—a family member or friend who's not afraid to tell you the truth. Do you tend to find the bad even in the greatest of situations, and to overlook the good?

This kind of attitude not only brings you down, but it also brings down those around you. It's hard to be happy in the presence of someone who is rarely if ever happy herself. So if you think it's *at all* possible that your negative attitude is stealing the joy God has tried to shower you with, get on your knees before Him (whether figuratively or literally) and ask Him if this is you.

Psalm 51:6 tells us that God desires truth in our inner being and will teach us wisdom in the deepest parts of ourselves. Be brave enough to ask Him this question and to hear His answer. You can't lose. Because even if He tells you that yes, part of your lack of joy is your own fault, at least you know what to do about it! You can ask Him to change your heart so that instead of looking for the bad, you look for the joy in any situation. Just think of all the joy that would be available to you if you got your own negative attitude out of the way!

By the way, this applies to all of us at times. All of us have moments when our own negative attitude steals our joy. I'm sure Satan's thrilled when this happens. We save him the trouble of having to steal it from us by stealing it from ourselves. Don't do this any longer, precious mom. Trade your negative attitude for the joy of the Lord!

Abundant Living Action Steps

1. What reasons for joy do you have in your life right now? Write each one on a card and stick it someplace where you'll see it later. Then, each time you see it, thank God for it.

2. Do you ever steal your own joy by being a negative person? Ask God to show you a time recently when you did that. Then ask Him to keep you from stealing your own joy.

For a more in-depth study of the topics of each chapter, see the Bible study at the end of this book.

Abundant Strength

You try to pay the bills,
you try to keep your life going
and there's pressure.
CARNIE WILSON

Being under pressure.

As moms, we understand what this is like. That's because whatever our circumstances, we as moms will be under pressure. Pressures from within, pressures from without—you name it. Sometimes it seems that being a mom is filled with pressure.

I asked a group of friends and readers to share times and ways in which they need strength as moms. These are some of the responses:

"Patience! I'm pretty sure if it wasn't for strength in patience I would have a head full of gray hair and a few heart attacks by now."

"Strength to turn my children over to God and stay out of the way. We trust God with our eternal soul, yet it can be terrifying to turn over our children . . . like we ever 'owned' them to start with?"

"Reining in my temper. It can be hard to not let the little ones (or spouses) push our buttons!"

"When our babies get sick."

"Continually refining my parenting skills with the goal of providing him the best possible environment in which he can develop."

"All of them. Patience, gentleness and compassion spring immediately to mind."

"Strength to outlast the kids' persistence!"

I would include a few more: When we haven't had much sleep. When we're having a bad day anyway. When we have to keep going and we. just. can't.

In this chapter, we're going to look at the strength God has given us to deal with all the pressures we face. But first, we need to look at what those pressures are and understand them a little better.

Two Kinds of Pressure

The responses above can be divided into two main categories: internal and external pressures. Internal pressures are those pressures we place upon ourselves. They're the ones that come from our beliefs about who we should be as moms, women and people. These beliefs are usually formed in a number of ways: from the input we got from our parents and others during childhood, from the input we get now, and from our own unique personalities convincing us that we "should" be this or that.

Sometimes, we're correct—we *should* be loving and kind, for example. But the pressure comes in when we convince ourselves that we should be able to do it all the time if we just try hard enough.

Or yes, we should be patient. But the pressure comes from expecting ourselves to be able to be patient on little sleep and when we're having a bad day, just by trying harder.

Likewise, some of the external pressures—those that come from outside of us—are accurate, and some are not. We feel external pressure to pay our bills, and yes, we should do that if we don't want the electricity or the water cut off. (Plus, we should make good on our debts when we owe the money.)

Sometimes, we also feel external pressure from other people, such as family, friends or even strangers, who believe they know what we should do and how we should do it. They may very well place all kinds of pressure on us to try to make us conform to what they think we should do or be. We can either allow the pressure to remain external—in other words, coming only from other people—or we can internalize it—that is, take it into ourselves and agree with them, and then begin to put pressure on ourselves to do whatever it is they want.

Pressure is primarily internal or external (or sometimes both), but it can take many forms. It can come from people, from laws, or from personal opinions. It can come from our children, from our physical health, or from the government. Whatever form pressure takes, it's something we have to deal with.

Dealing with Pressure

Most of us have a preferred strategy for dealing with pressure. Some of us tend to stuff it inside until we either get depressed or explode—or both. Others of us head straight for the depression or the explosion. Still others of us react to pressure by pushing back against it. And others of us simply shut down in the face of pressure.

In other words, we don't always choose a godly response to pressure.

What would a healthy, godly response look like? That's the problem. We don't always know. We're not sure what we should do in a given situation. So instead of acting, we simply *react*. We don't know how to choose something different.

Let's talk about how to do that. Let's talk about strategies for dealing with the varied kinds of pressure we face as moms. As we talk about each strategy, we'll see how God has given us the strength to carry it out. In fact, He has poured incredibly abundant strength into our lives, if we know how to take advantage of it.

Taking the Burden to God

I have to confess something to you: I'm not always great in this area. God frequently has to remind me to bring my burdens to Him, even though doing so is something I should think about as a first option, not as a last option:

Let me also tell you something else: Bringing our burdens to God doesn't result in all of our problems immediately going away and everything in our lives being better.

I hate it when someone says, "Well, just give it to God," as a pat answer, as if doing so should make all my stress and negative feelings go away. As if it's just that simple. But I have learned that whether someone tells me this as a pat answer or not, that person is usually right—I usually haven't been giving my problems to God.

What does it mean to give a problem to God? What does it mean to take a burden to Him, and how can we do it?

What it means is that when we're feeling stressed and need strength, we discuss it with God. We come before Him and pour out our hearts in the matter. We not only ask Him what to do, but we also ask Him what His will is in the matter. We make seeking Him and His perspective a priority. We ask for His strength and peace. We do this repeatedly, for as long as it takes.

Most of us find it easier to call a girlfriend or take our problems to someone over email or via Facebook than to take our problems to God. We know what it means to give our problems to someone else, because we give them to other *people* all the time. It seems harder to know exactly how to give problems to God, because we can't hear His voice in a back-and-forth conversation the same way we can another human being's.

But oh, are we ever making a big mistake if we think that, ultimately, other people can give us more help than God can. Yes, absolutely, we should seek the counsel of others. Proverbs 11:14 tells us that there is victory when we have plenty of (good, godly) counselors. But we shouldn't seek the counsel of fallible human beings, who have only limited knowledge, to the exclusion of seeking God's counsel.

Take your problems to Him. Do it as many times as it takes, for as long as it takes. Make God a priority, not a last-ditch effort when your friends don't know how to help you. He's probably not going to force His counsel upon you. He's ready and willing to give you His strength when you need it, but He won't force that on you, either. He'll give it when you ask, but that's the thing: You have to ask, and you have to be serious about it.

So yes, seek the counsel of family and friends. But above all, seek God's counsel. He is the one who can truly strengthen you to deal with the pressure you face.

Consider Whether the Pressure Is Legitimate

By this, I mean that we need to look at the nature of the pressure we are experiencing. Is it legitimate? Is it coming from a legitimate source? Is it perhaps legitimate pressure, but not to the extent to which we're feeling it?

As moms, we tend to take on far too many things. Not just activities that fill up our schedules, but responsibilities as well as beliefs about how we should act in particular circumstances. We need to stop and consider whether or not the pressure we're feeling is legitimate.

For example, when I was a new mom, I felt incredible pressure to do everything right. I wanted so badly to be a great parent that I put an amazing amount of pressure on myself to find that one right way to do everything—and then to do it perfectly.

Was this pressure legitimate? No.

It's true that we should do our best to be great moms. That's 100 percent, absolutely true. But the idea that there's one right way to do things? Wrong. The idea that I could somehow do everything right if I just tried hard enough? Also wrong.

Putting this kind of pressure on myself came from my perfectionistic tendencies. I knew that. But it was hard to stop. Stopping has been a learned skill for me—something I have had to work on doing.

I remember a time, during my "new mom" season, when a friend of mine came over. She has six children, and she visited me regularly to mentor me as I began walking through the stages of parenting. I was lamenting to her one day that my house never seemed clean and I never seemed to be able to get everything done like I had before.

"Megan," she said, looking straight at me, "you're going to have to lower your standards."

"*Lower* my standards?" I asked incredulously.

"Yes, *lower* them," she said. "You can't possibly do everything perfectly. No matter how hard you try, there are going to be times when you simply can't get everything done. You're going to have to lower your standards so that you can be satisfied with what's realistic, instead of what's perfection."

I thought about her words for a long time. (Actually, 11 years later, I still think about them from time to time.) I realized that she was right. My friend wasn't telling me that I shouldn't strive for a clean house. She was simply telling me that I needed to be realistic about what was possible to accomplish and what wasn't.

Then, if something wasn't possible, I needed to take the pressure to do it off of myself. (We'll talk more about this in the next section.)

So how far do I lower my standards? you might wonder. *If I lower them too far, isn't that bad?*

Yes, lowering standards too far is bad. But here's the great thing: God has given you guidelines for what kind of standards you should try to maintain. He will tell you when you're putting too much pressure on yourself (sometimes He does this by allowing you to feel that feeling of stress). One of the ways He gives you strength is by giving you reasonable standards that you *can* meet. Even when you're tired. Even when you're having a bad day. Even when you're confused or worn out or overwhelmed.

And God's standard is simply this: Do the best you can (see Col. 3:23). He doesn't say, *"Be perfect."* (Well, He does, but it's in a different context where He's talking about being morally perfect.)

He doesn't say, *"Be able to do everything that needs to be done, no matter what."* He simply says, *"Do your best. Work with all your heart."*

That, precious mom, is a standard we can all attain. We can do our best. We don't have to "do perfection."

Even when you're tired, you can meet this standard. True, your tired best might not look as good as your energetic best, but it doesn't have to. Your had-a-bad-day best won't look as perky as your everything's-right-with-the-world best. That's okay. It doesn't have to look a certain way. It just has to be the best you can give at that moment in time. You see? God has strengthened you by enabling you to meet His standards. Not illegitimate standards that come from elsewhere. *His* standards.

Just do your best. That's all He asks.

Take the Pressure Off

Let's get back to what my friend said: "Lower your standards."

She was talking about taking the pressure off when the goal was impossible to achieve anyway. I would add that we need to take the pressure off when it's illegitimate pressure—when it's pressure other than to be and to do our best—or when it comes from an illegitimate source.

Many times, we act as if we *must* comply with whatever pressure is placed upon us. I'm not sure where we get that idea, but it's completely false. It doesn't matter who is putting this pressure on you. If you've taken it before God, and this pressure is not something you need to be dealing with or comply with, remove it! Tell yourself you're not going to allow someone else to place a burden upon you that's greater than the tasks God has placed upon you.

I know it can be difficult. When the person who is pressuring you won't let up, or if it is someone close to you, refusing to succumb to the pressure can be hard. But remember that we are not to worship any other gods.

What does worshiping other gods have to do with it? Simply this: When we allow someone else to place a command upon us that God does not want us to follow, we put that person in the position of God.

We begin to worship that other person's will instead of God's will. That's idolatry!

Yes, other people have a right to ask us to do things for them. But when we put other people in charge of our lives, especially if we do so in ways that are contrary to what God wants for our lives, we are committing idolatry.

You may never have thought about it that way before, but it's true. Putting anything or anybody in God's place when they're not really God is displacing the One who really *is* God. Don't do it, my friend. Resist the temptation to cave in to people who don't want what God wants for you. Let God be the one who determines what's best for your life.

Other people might place burdens on you that you were never meant to bear. God won't. Nor will He place burdens on you that are too heavy. If a burden is too heavy for you, perhaps you should consider whether God is really asking you to bear this burden, or whether you have allowed someone else (possibly yourself!) to weigh you down with stuff God never wanted you to worry about.

God will give you the ability to resist illegitimate pressure, if you ask Him. He knows that when you take on goals He never meant for you to have, you are veering off the path of abundant life. Only God knows exactly what should constitute abundant life for you. Let Him be the one to determine it.

Pressures We Face as Moms

So, what about the legitimate pressures we face as moms? Pressures that we know are God's will, but which still seem hard to bear?

For me, one of those pressures is cooking. I don't like to cook. Under other circumstances, I might kind of enjoy it, but when I have five children clamoring for my attention and myriad other things to do, I don't find it enjoyable at all. Yet I know that it is God's will for me to provide food for my children. How do I do it?

Or how can you and I be patient when the kids are on our *last* nerve? How can we respond patiently instead of biting their poor little heads off?

How can we be kind and loving when what we're really feeling is selfish? How can we put our children ahead of ourselves when we barely have enough strength to get ourselves through the day, much less to handle little people?

First, those of us who are particularly prone to perfectionism will need to ask God to help us lower our standards appropriately and give ourselves some grace. But if it's not a matter of needing to adjust our perspective or take the pressure off—if it's a matter of truly needing strength to do something God legitimately asks us to do—we must ask for His strength.

Sound too simplistic? It's not. It's just that simple, and that's part of the beauty of it. You see, God meets our needs when we ask. Often, He meets our needs even when we don't ask. But sometimes, He waits for us to ask before He supplies what we need (see Jas. 4:2).

This is particularly true with strength. God will generally not force His strength upon us. He usually gives it to us when we're interested. If we'd rather try to do everything on our own—in our own power—and exhaust ourselves, He'll let us. But it doesn't have to be that way. We can ask for His strength.

Just as Christ gives peace that passes understanding, He also gives strength that passes understanding. I can't explain how this strength works. I can only tell you that whenever I've asked Him to, God has strengthened me, both by His presence and by His strength that He imparts.

Let's look at a few verses that demonstrate what I'm talking about:

The LORD is my strength and my shield; my heart trusts in him, and I am helped. My heart leaps for joy and I will give thanks to him in song (Ps. 28:7, *NIV*).

God is our refuge and strength, an ever-present help in
trouble (Ps. 46:1, *NIV*).

My flesh and my heart may fail, but God is the strength of
my heart and my portion forever (Ps. 73:26, *NIV*).

"My flesh and my heart may fail." Do you ever feel like that,
moms? We all do. But notice what comes next: "God is the strength
of my heart and my portion forever."

How long will He be enough for us? Forever. Not just a little
while. Not just while this crisis is in full swing. But forever.

That's abundant life, my friends. Strength *forever*, to bear whatever may come. God Himself being our strength—and since we
know He will never leave us, we'll have Him as our strength at
any moment.

But sometimes we still feel so weak. What about those times?

The apostle Paul explains, "That is why, for Christ's sake, I delight in weaknesses, in insults, in hardships, in persecutions, in difficulties. For when I am weak, then I am strong" (2 Cor. 12:10, *NIV*).

Even when we're weak according to human standards, we can
be strong according to God's standards. And remember what we've
said in this chapter—that God's standards are the important ones.

Fortunately, He gives us the strength to meet them. That's a
huge part of the abundant life we have in Him.

Abundant Living Action Steps

1. In what ways do you need strength as a mom? List them. Then ask God for His help with each one.
2. Look in your Bible's concordance for verses that have to do with strength. Choose a few that are most meaningful to you and post them around your house, where you can see them and be encouraged.

For a more in-depth study of the topics of each chapter, see the Bible study at the end of this book.

Part 3

Changing
Your
Perspective

Become Last

The natural state of motherhood is unselfishness.
When you become a mother, you are no longer the center of your
own universe. You relinquish that position to your children.
JESSICA LANGE

On my bookshelf sits a small decoration on a rectangular base. On the base are the figures of Jesus and Peter; Jesus is kneeling to wash Peter's feet.

I have this decoration in an easily visible place to remind me what my role in my children's lives is. Yes, I am to guide them, direct them, and sometimes give them commands. But I am also to be their servant.

Jesus said, "If anyone wants to be first, he must be the very last, and the servant of all" (Mark 9:35, *NIV*).

Ouch. Sometimes that's hard. Really hard.

I can remember times when I started to tell my children, "I'm not your . . ." and had to stop myself because yes, I am their servant. I also remember a time when I was still working while pregnant with Ellie, and the people I was working for were being pretty demanding.

"What am I, your servant?" I grumbled to myself.

God stopped me cold. "Yes," He said. "You *are* their servant."

He was right.

The pastor at a church of which we were formerly members used to say (and presumably still does), "You'll know whether or not you truly have a servant heart by your reaction to being treated like a servant."

These words have stayed with me, because I have to admit that sometimes, being a servant is difficult for me. Sometimes, I would rather do just about anything than have to serve one more person, one more time. But the fact remains that I am to be my children's servant, even if I don't always have a servant's heart—which, by the way, is my choice.

Sometimes, we don't have a servant's heart. Sometimes, we don't even know what it would mean in a particular situation to have one. So let's start there—by looking at what it means to have a servant's heart. We'll also look at what in the world a servant's heart has to do with abundant life.

A Servant's Heart

Let's go back and revisit Mark 9:35 for a minute: "If anyone wants to be first, he must be the very last, and the servant of all" (*NIV*). Jesus was saying that if anyone wants to be truly great, he must be willing to be a servant. A servant's heart, then, is a heart that is willing and eager to fulfill this teaching.

In other words, if we have a servant's heart, we will not only be willing to serve others, but we will also *want* to do so. We'll be glad to do it when we get the opportunity. We won't do it grudgingly or resentfully; we'll do it joyfully.

Wow. Some days, I definitely do not have a servant's heart.

There are days when I find it difficult to serve my children. There are days when I want to be the one who's served. Maybe I'm sick or tired, or maybe I just want a little attention. I want others to serve me. And yes, everyone in a house should serve the others. But this verse doesn't say I should be the servant of all "sometimes." The implication is pretty clear that I should be a servant all the time, not just when I might be in a good mood and feel like it.

At one time, one of my children seemed to be stuck in a habit of wanting to know why he or she should have to clean up messes he or she didn't make. I got tired of being asked "Why?" so one day, I said, "You know what? Let's have a day where we don't have to do anything we don't want to do."

"Really?" that child said. "Will I get in trouble?"

"No, you won't get in trouble," I said. "You don't have to do anything you don't want to do today."

"Okay," the child agreed.

Everything went fine until suppertime. "I'm hungry," my child said.

"I'm sorry," I said. "I don't feel like fixing dinner."

"But. . . but . . ."

"Remember? Today we're not doing anything we don't want to do."

"But *you* can't do that!"

"Sure I can," I said. "Either we all pitch in, or nobody has to do anything."

That child has never again asked why he or she has to clean up somebody else's mess.

This worked well as an example for my child (helping to develop his or her little servant's heart). It doesn't work so well when I act as if it's true all the time—that I don't have to do what I don't want to do.

By contrast, if I have a servant's heart, even when I don't particularly enjoy the task, I will want to meet my loved one's needs and be willing to do what needs to be done.

What does a servant's heart have to do with abundant life? Simply this: If I'm willing to be a servant, I won't get bogged down in resenting all the times I have to serve. Instead, I'll actually get joy from them and maybe even look forward to them. There's no question that as a mom, I have plenty of opportunities to serve, so having a true servant's heart would make me glad just about all the time.

If we don't have a servant's heart at present, we can ask God to change us. After all, He is the Master at changing hearts!

Giving Up Rights

Becoming last—being a servant—involves giving up some of our rights. In this section, we're going to talk about three rights we have to give up if we are to be true servants. As always, we'll also talk about what this has to do with abundant life!

The first right we give up as servants is the right to direct our own actions. Servants have masters. Or, in our case, a Master. He is the one who gets to direct our actions, not us.

To be clear, our children are not our masters. We have one Master—God. He has chosen, at this time in our lives, to direct our actions toward serving our children.

Does that mean that He's dooming us to a life that's less than abundant? Not at all! He's actually showing us the way to abundant life. One way we get a glimpse of what abundant life is all about is through serving others.

For one thing, serving others means that we have a reason to serve. We'll touch on this more in a later chapter, but the very fact that we have kids to serve means that our lives are abundant. Instead of resenting the fact that we have to serve, we should rejoice in the truth that our lives are so abundant that they give us a reason to serve.

There are many people who would love to have children to serve, but they don't. Maybe they've never been able to have children; maybe one or more of their children has died. Those folks would give anything to be able to serve their children. Yet we complain about serving ours.

Sometimes, we're just plain worn out or burnt out. I understand that. But even in those times, we can choose to be grateful that we have children to serve—and grateful for the chance to do something for them.

When I had my first daughter, a friend from church gave me two books about motherhood. In the first one, the author gave this example: Say you are lying in bed, and you hear your child coughing. You might lie there and think, *Please, God, let her stop coughing so I don't have to get up.*

That's normal. All moms understand this. But as the author pointed out, another possible response would be, *Thank You, God, that I have this child to serve. Thank You that I am able to be here for her now and to go serve her.*

Sound incredible? It did to me too. But the point the author was trying to make is this: We have a choice about our attitude. We may not be able to choose whether or not we feel tired, but we can choose the attitude with which we get up to serve.

For another thing, serving means that we have the ability to serve. A healthy body and the ability to carry out our service are no small things for which to be thankful. We could choose, every time we have the chance to serve someone, to be thankful for the ability to do the service. We could be thankful for our legs that will carry us into the kitchen, for our arms and hands that will help us prepare the meal, and for the strength to put it on the table. We could see each act of service as a chance for rejoicing instead of resentment. Wouldn't our lives be much more abundant if we looked at things that way?

A second right we have to give up is the right to be the center of attention. As our quotation at the beginning of this chapter reminded us, once we become moms, it's not all about us anymore.

Maybe when we were growing up, it was more about us. We were the children, after all. Then, when we became engaged, it was still about us, because we were the brides-to-be. As newlyweds, it was still all about us, as our husbands did their best to please us and others congratulated us. When we became pregnant or began the process of adoption, it was *still* about us, as we became the expectant mothers.

But then, when that baby was born or that child was placed in our arms . . . well, suddenly it wasn't all about us anymore. It was about the children. And it can be hard—really hard—to give up being the center of attention.

For some of us, this is particularly challenging. Some of us love to be the center of attention. So the comedown to a place where we are no longer the focus of everything, even in our own household, can be difficult. Putting another person first means, by definition, putting ourselves second. (Or at least, we hope for second. Sometimes it feels more like tenth or hundredth.)

So how does giving up our right to be the center of attention lead to abundant life? Doesn't it just mean that our lives will get less and less abundant as we fade into obscurity?

Not at all! Because in giving the center of attention to someone else, we will be farther along the road to discovering what it truly means to be a servant. Remember how we said that serving others is abundant life? Well then, humbling ourselves to second (or lower) place is one quick step on the road to abundant life.

Not only that, but Matthew 23:12 tells us that whoever exalts himself—puts himself first and highest—will be humbled, and whoever humbles himself (puts himself second) will be exalted. This doesn't mean that we'll never have to serve again, but it does mean that we'd be wise to humble ourselves so that God doesn't have to do it for us.

Third, if we want to become servants, we must give up our right to be served. A servant doesn't get to sit around being served; he or she is the one who must do the serving. That pretty well describes the life of a mom, doesn't it? Doing the serving?

So if we want to be true servants, we must give up our right to be served. Give up our right to make sure we get our needs met when and how we want them met. We must accept the fact that there will be times when our needs and desires get met later than we wanted, if they get met at all. And we must be okay with that.

So how in the world does *this* lead to abundant life? Doesn't it just mean that we're doomed to run on empty for the rest of our lives?

No way! For remember that Jesus said that whoever wanted to save his life (in other words, whoever wanted to make sure all his needs got met when and how he wanted) would lose it, but whoever was willing to lose his life (to become a servant) would find it (see Mark 8:35). Finding true life is hardly what I would call a net loss. It's a gain, and a huge one, because it shows us the way to abundant life.

Who knew that being a servant was actually part of God's means to an end—the end being abundant life? It is. It truly is.

Refuse to become a servant, and you will lose your life. Develop a servant's heart, and you will save your life.

Which option sounds more abundant to you?

Abundant Living Action Steps

1. Is it a challenge for you to serve others with a willing heart? Why or why not? If it is, ask God to change your heart. (See Ps. 51:10.)
2. What does your attitude toward serving need to look like? How would this be a change from your current attitude? Write out your answers to these questions.

For a more in-depth study of the topics of each chapter, see the Bible study at the end of this book.

See Your Children as Blessings

Without my children, my house would be clean and
my wallet would be full, but my heart would be empty.
ANONYMOUS

"Children are a blessing from the Lord."

We've heard this statement in sermons; people have told us this; and we know the Bible tells us so (see Ps. 127:3). We even believe it—to a certain extent.

That is, we believe it when our children are acting right and everything is going smoothly. Maybe someone even tells us what a blessing our children are, and we nod and say to ourselves, *Yep, they sure are.*

But the next day, when the kids have spent the whole day bickering and being slow to obey, we remember the conversation from the day before, and we think, *Blessing? Maybe so, but it sure doesn't feel like it sometimes.*

That's because as moms—even as loving moms—it can be easier for us to call to mind all the trouble we go to on behalf of our kids (or all the trouble they cause us) than it is to remember the many blessings we enjoy because of our children day in and day out.

Many of us have a tendency to focus on the negative or the imperfect when it comes to our children. I observed this on one occasion when my husband and I were waiting to be seated at a restaurant (yes, it was an actual date!). Sitting next to us in the waiting area were a mother and her little girl. The little girl was getting restless waiting, which was understandable. When you're two or three, waiting 20 minutes in an unfamiliar place with no toys seems like an eternity.

But as far as her mom was concerned, that little girl couldn't do anything right.

After 10 minutes of criticizing her child for everything she could think of, the mom finally turned to us and said, "If I'd known she was going to be like this, I wouldn't have had her."

I've heard many people say something like that in jest. But this mom didn't sound like she was joking. And every negative thing she said, she said well within the child's hearing and understanding.

I don't know that mom's circumstances. Maybe she had had a bad day. Maybe something else had gone on that made her super-sensitive to every little thing the girl did. I don't know. But I do know that instead of focusing on what a delightful little girl she had (and the rest of us sitting there were truly delighted with her), she was focusing on what she perceived as the negative.

I could only imagine what her words did to that little girl's spirit. And I can only imagine what our words do to our children when we say things that indicate that we see them as burdens rather than blessings.

I don't want to hurt my child's soul by having the wrong focus. Scripture makes it clear that if my perspective is wrong, eventually, hurtful words will come out of my mouth (see, for example, Matt. 12:34). I know you don't want to do that either. So let's look at three reasons to believe that our children are blessings, even when they may be driving us crazy.

God Says Our Children Are Blessings

Psalm 127:3 tells us, "Sons [and daughters] are a heritage from the LORD, children a reward from him" (*NIV*).

Notice that word "reward." Children aren't just something mediocre given as leftovers; they are a reward. In other words, they're blessings. We know this because God says so.

Yet too often we look to circumstances to determine whether or not we feel blessed by our children. Some days we do; some days we don't. We give circumstances a higher authority than we give God's Word in establishing what is and is not a blessing. This is not the perspective of a mom who truly believes that her children are a reward and a blessing.

Aren't you glad our heavenly Father doesn't wait until we're perfect before He decides that we are blessings? If He did, He would never term us blessings. He'd call us a burden. If the infinitely perfect God not merely tolerates but also rejoices in His imperfect children, why do we not rejoice in ours?

True, God doesn't rejoice in our sins, and He doesn't expect us to rejoice in our children's sins, either. But He does indeed rejoice in *us*. In fact, Zephaniah 3:17 says that God takes great delight in us and rejoices over us. This is not the perspective of someone who requires that His children be perfect in order to term them blessings. This is the perspective of a Father who loves His children *so much* that no matter what they do, He loves them deeply and passionately.

God doesn't just love us passionately when we're behaving ourselves. Good thing, too, or there would be portions of every day and night when He didn't love us. He loves us all the time. This is the same kind of love we need to extend to our children—a love that assures them that no matter what they do, they are a blessing to us, and we want them to know it.

Children Really Are Blessings

It's true. Children bring with them far more blessings than we can count. They bless us every single day.

For example, today my 16-month-old son snuggled up to me before his naptime. He didn't want any gifts from me. He didn't want me to do anything for him. He just wanted *me*. And I was blessed.

Also today, seven-year-old Lindsey came to where I was sitting (working on this book) and waited quietly by my side. I came to a good stopping spot, turned to her, and asked, "What do you need?"

"I just want to be with you," she said.

I was blessed.

You can probably think of many similar moments when your kids have done things that warmed your heart. Maybe they snuggled up next to you. Maybe they made you a precious gift.

Or maybe it wasn't something they did. Maybe you were blessed just by smelling the sweet smell of their hair after a bath or hearing their infectious giggle over something silly.

Whatever the means, children bring countless blessings into our lives every day.

Things We Wouldn't Have Known Otherwise

Not the least of the blessings our children bring to us is that, because of them, we get to know people we wouldn't have gotten to know otherwise. For example, I have a dear friend in Georgia named Rebekah whom I met when I spoke at her church. If I had never had children, I would not have begun a motherhood-based ministry, and I probably never would have met Rebekah.

Likewise, I met my best friend, Lori, at a ballet class my daughter was attending. Obviously, if I hadn't had children, I wouldn't have been at the class, and I may very well never have met Lori.

Who are the people in your life whom you probably never would have met if you didn't have children? These friends are additional blessings your children have brought into your life.

Knowing Yourself

Not only that, but you wouldn't have known yourself in the same way that you do now. You wouldn't have seen yourself grow and mature in quite the same way. You would never have needed to make the changes in your character that you've made because you have children. You might never have realized that you were selfish, or that you get really crabby when deprived of sleep long-term, had you not had children.

So not only are your children blessings because God says so, because they truly are blessings, and because they introduce you to people you never would have met otherwise, but they are also blessings because they help you become a person you never could have been otherwise.

And you're better for it. I've never heard someone say, "You know, I think I'm a worse person now that I'm a mom." No, but over and over, I've heard women say, "I've changed so much since becoming a mom. I'm a much better person now."

Moms, with children pouring blessings into our lives every day just by their very existence, we experience abundant life in a way we wouldn't have had we not become mothers. True, we wouldn't have encountered some of the things that drive us crazy, but neither would we have encountered many of the things that fill our hearts to overflowing.

Abundant life because of your children, mom. What greater gift could they give you?

But there's more. Because something every mom needs to realize is that it's a privilege to have children at all.

Our Story

My husband and I got married on December 16, 1995. We waited a couple years, and then we decided that we were ready for kids. The only problem was that we couldn't seem to conceive.

Every month, we were hopeful. And every month, we got the same answer.

No. Not pregnant. Not this month.

Finally, we sought medical advice, and we were told that without medical intervention, we would probably never have children. "I can't say never," the doctor said. "But . . ." and he shrugged.

Why didn't it work for us? we wondered. Why could 12-year-olds have babies and leave them in trash bins (a story that happened in a neighboring community), and we couldn't have a baby at all?

We prayed, cried and agonized over not being able to conceive. During this time, we pursued a private adoption, which fell through at the last minute when the birth mother decided to keep her baby. We grieved deeply over not being able to adopt. Finally, we decided to pursue medical options to see if we could have our own biological children. If not, we would willingly try again to adopt.

You know the rest of the story. The medical interventions worked, and we now have five children. But for the first seven-and-a-half years of our marriage, we had none. Zero. Not a single one. And we didn't know if there would ever be any.

During that long season of waiting, I promised God that if He ever let me have children, I would not forget what it was like to want children and not be able to have them. He did let me have children, and I have kept my promise never to forget.

I know what it's like to hear people complain about their children and to think, *At least you* have *children.* I know what it's like to grieve so heavily that it's hard to be sympathetic toward a pregnant friend who constantly complains about the difficulties of her pregnancy—because at least she's pregnant.

So for those of us who do have children, whether through birth or adoption, I want us to remember that it's a privilege to have those children. There are some women who want desperately to be moms and can't. They would love to have the struggles we have with our kids.

I know the fact that other women want children and don't have them doesn't make our struggles any easier. But perhaps it can help us adjust our perspective enough that we don't focus on the negative instead of the blessings involved in having children.

Likewise, I have a dear friend whose son died in infancy. She would give anything for him to still be alive, but she doesn't get that choice. She doesn't get to experience the blessings of watching him grow and become the man he could have been. Her loss has caused me to rethink my complaints about my children.

Yes, my children sometimes drive me crazy. But at least I have children. At least they're here.

Their being here is a large part of what makes my life abundant.

Abundant Living Action Points

1. Write down at least five reasons that each of your children is a blessing to you.
2. Do you know someone who is struggling with infertility or child/infant loss? Why not reach out to that person today?

For a more in-depth study of the topics of each chapter, see the Bible study at the end of this book.

18

Come Alongside Others

I alone cannot change the world,
but I can cast a stone across the waters to create many ripples.
MOTHER TERESA

One time a few years ago, when two of my children were in pre-school, I went to pick them up. It was a rainy, gray day, and I could barely get into the building without getting soaked in the process. I decided that we wouldn't go to the library after all, as the kids had been expecting, because I didn't want to try to get four kids (the number we had at the time) into and out of the library without somebody getting drenched. There was no way I was even going to attempt that. We'd just go home and find something to do there.

I entered Lindsey's classroom and saw that another mother had arrived ahead of me. She was kneeling in front of her son, helping him fasten his coat. As I greeted Lindsey, I heard this oth-er mom say sweetly, "Yeah, it's a yucky day out. So we're going to put up a tent in the living room and pretend like we're camping. We can even eat marshmallows!"

I stopped and looked at her for a moment. Inwardly, I was thinking, *Come on, lady, you're making the rest of us look bad here.*

Almost immediately, I felt guilty for my thoughts. Just because another mom had an idea that I didn't, was willing to see a neg-ative for a positive, and was willing to put forth more effort than I was was no reason for me to secretly roll my eyes and call her an overachiever. I could have done any one of the things she did. But because I didn't think of it, and because I probably would have

taken the easy way out if I had, I cut down this other mom (even
if she didn't know it) so that I wouldn't feel so bad for not doing
for my children what she was going to do for hers.

But here's the thing, moms: We aren't in competition with
one another. We're supposed to be in community, not competition. We're supposed to build each other up and share ideas, not
cut each other down. We have a marvelous group of women with
whom to be in community, if we just understand what community
is supposed to be like.

We're Not in Competition

Rachel and Leah understood all about competition.

You know Rachel and Leah, the biological mothers of most of
the patriarchs (and the legal mothers of all of them) who became
the fathers of the twelve tribes of Israel. Rachel and Leah were
competitive to a fault.

We find their story in Genesis. In order to understand why
they were in such competition, we need to take some background
into account.

As the result of a major (and I do mean major) family fight at
home, Jacob came to work for his Uncle Laban. While there, he met
his cousins Leah and Rachel. Rachel was beautiful, and Jacob fell
in love with her. In fact, he was so smitten that he agreed to work
seven years for Laban in exchange for Rachel's hand in marriage (a
commitment far beyond the usual bride price). Jacob did, in fact,
work seven years, and at the end of that time, there was a wedding.

The only problem was that Jacob married the wrong woman.

Yeah. Oops.

Back in that time, the bride would have worn veils. Perhaps
these helped to disguise the fact that it was Leah he was marrying
instead of Rachel. (Rachel and Leah's father, who was trying to get
Leah married off, was in on the whole deal.) It's also possible that
Jacob became drunk at the wedding celebration, and maybe that
dulled his senses.

Whatever the explanation, the fact remains that after the wedding night, Jacob woke up next to the wrong woman. As he was legally married to her, there wasn't much he could do to fix the situation.

The only thing he could do was agree to work another seven years for Rachel, the bride he had wanted in the first place. After a week, Jacob married Rachel too, and then he served another seven years for her.

It was during this time that the competition between the sisters became evident. Probably it had started even before, when it first became obvious that Jacob had eyes for Rachel. But here is where we first hear of the competition: "When the LORD saw that Leah was hated, he opened her womb, but Rachel was barren" (Gen. 29:31).

Okay, so now we know that Leah was hated. It's no small wonder, considering the deception in which she participated. But because she was hated, probably by her husband as well as by her sister, the Lord had pity on her and allowed her to bear a son.

She went on to bear him two more sons, for a total of three, all while Rachel was still barren. "Maybe now my husband will love me," she speculated, "because I have borne him three sons" (see Gen. 29:34). Not only did she bear him those three sons, but she also bore him a fourth before she temporarily stopped being able to have children. (She later went on to have two more sons and a daughter, for a total of six sons and one daughter.)

Genesis 30 tells us that when Rachel saw Leah having children, she was envious of her sister, and she sent her maid to have sex with Jacob. If the maid conceived, the child would legally be Rachel's. This was the competition. The sisters were trying to one-up each other by having more children than the other. What would be the payoff? Jacob's love. Talk about fighting over a man. Talk about competition. Conceiving children just to win your husband's favor or prove that you were better than your sister. Sad.

The way we moms sometimes compete with each other today is equally sad.

Sometimes we compete in the same way: by trying to have more children than another mom. Maybe we think this will make us look better than she does; maybe we simply want to have something she doesn't have or can't have. But having children to compete with another mom is ridiculous. Children should be conceived out of love, not out of jealousy or ambition.

We also compete by tearing other moms down. After all, if they're brought down, we'll be higher than they are, right? We'll be superior.

You may *appear* superior to another mom you're tearing down, but that doesn't mean you *are* superior. God is the one who's the judge of that, and He has already said that He loves all His children. He's also given us plenty of guidelines for how to treat one another, including loving one another and restoring one another when necessary. Nowhere does He say that we should tear others down to make ourselves feel good.

Along the same lines, most of us are pretty good (or pretty bad, depending on how you look at it) at being judgmental. We judge other moms for what they do, without knowing all the circumstances.

Let's say, for example, that you're at Target. You see a mom in the next aisle whose son is having a meltdown. "I want it!" he screams.

You know the story. The mom resists for a while, but finally, she gives in and buys the toy so her child will stop screaming about it.

As soon as this happens, we begin judging the other mom. *She shouldn't have done that. She should have just walked away.*

Maybe those things are true, but then again, maybe they're not. It could be that the child has special needs and that the mother is dealing with him the best way she knows how. True, the odds aren't in favor of that explanation, but see how quick we are to assume we know exactly what's going on and that we can make judgments about what another mom could have or should have done?

We usually don't stop there. Once we've judged the mom's actions, we move on to start judging *her. She probably doesn't discipline him at all*, we think to ourselves (or maybe say to a girlfriend later), the implication in our minds being: *and she's not a very good mother*.

We also judge moms who work outside the home, or who don't; moms who choose public school, or moms who homeschool; and moms who do or don't allow certain things in their homes. We're quick to judge because we think we have enough knowledge to make that judgment.

But even if we do—even if we're right—our judgments usually don't lead to our helping the other mom out. They usually lead to our condemning her, rather than trying to do something positive to help in the situation, or at least sympathizing with her in her struggle.

Why is this? Why are we so quick to judge other moms harshly?

Because we want to make ourselves feel better.

But, moms, there's a way to make ourselves feel better that's a whole lot, well, better, and that's this: to *help* the other mom instead of standing back and judging her. We could choose to be *with* her instead of *against* her. We could choose to be in community with her instead of deeming her an outsider because her actions don't live up to what we feel she should do.

We Are in Community

You see, we're in community with other moms. All other moms, all over the world. Moms from different cultures, or our own culture. Moms who are taller, shorter, bigger, skinnier, more talented, less talented, more energetic, less energetic—get the idea? We are a community of women who are bound together by at least one commonality, and that's that we have children.

There are at least two advantages to being in community with such a large group of women, and we'll talk about those in this section.

The first is that we are part of a group of people who all know how to help one another. That's because as moms, we understand what other moms need. We know what it's like to be up with a baby all night, to have to deal with the kids alone because our husband's gone (or we're single), and to try to figure out how in the world to discipline the child who just did the craziest thing.

Have you ever thought about that? That you are part of a worldwide community of moms who understand the same things you understand? And that these moms therefore know how to help you?

It's true that no other mom is the mother of your children, and that you are the one who has to make the decisions for your family. No other mom can parent your kids for you. But other moms can help you.

Maybe they can give you ideas; maybe they can bring you meals; maybe they can babysit your children for a while so that you can have some time to yourself. Maybe they can just be a listening ear for you when you need to vent about how hard things have been. After all, they can probably say, "Yep. I've been there."

We as moms desperately need a community like this. Of course, we still have to choose our friends carefully as well as choose carefully the people we allow to influence us most. It's to these moms that we will most often turn for advice. But even moms we barely know can sometimes offer insights or even encouragement when it's just been one of *those* days.

Another thing other moms can understand—whether moms you know well or moms you don't know at all—is what is important to you and what it feels like to have that incredible love for your kids that we talked about earlier. Other moms feel the same way about their kids that you do about yours. They know what it's like to be willing to sacrifice for your children, even to the extent of sacrificing your life.

I remember a time shortly after my younger sister had just become a mom. We were talking about the changes she had experienced since giving birth, and one thing amazed Kristen most of all. "Megan, I didn't know I could love anybody as much as I love Grace," she said.

All over the world, other moms understand loving their kids and putting them first. Other moms understand wanting the best for their children and being willing to do anything in their power to make that happen. Other moms understand how you feel as you wrestle over decisions that will make a big impact in your child's life, or even as you go to vote your conscience on issues that will deeply affect your children.

Moms, you are part of a community that understands not only the little things, but also the big things, and empathizes with you. This is an aspect of abundant life—being part of a whole group of people who understand you and validate you (even if they don't know you), and who share your experiences. As we participate in building one another up instead of tearing one another down—in understanding instead of judging—and as we receive help, hope and understanding from other moms, we find out more of what abundant life is all about.

Abundant Living Action Steps

1. Do you feel a need to be superior to other moms? How does this need express itself? Be honest before God and ask Him to forgive you. Also ask any mom you have wronged to forgive you.
2. Name a mom you know whom you could encourage this week. Make specific plans to bless her life.

For a more in-depth study of the topics of each chapter, see the Bible study at the end of this book.

MEGAN BREEDLOVE

Part 4

Practical

Abundance

Abundance in the Mind and Heart

My mother had a great deal of trouble with me, but I think she enjoyed it.
MARK TWAIN

So now we know. We know that abundance comes not from perfect circumstances but from knowing God Himself. Only He can truly satisfy us; only through Him will our lives be fully abundant.

But what does that look like in the heart and mind of a mom who sometimes feels overwhelmed? What about a mom who tends to compare herself to others? Or a mom who doesn't feel confident in her parenting choices? Who constantly questions herself as to whether she's doing the right thing, or doing it well enough?

We'll look at the answers to those questions for these three groups of moms. Because knowing God is not merely a spiritual exercise that has no practical benefits for living in today's world. It has very real and tangible benefits as we go through our days trying to figure out how to turn the chaos in our minds and hearts into abundance.

Feeling Overwhelmed

There isn't a mom on this planet who hasn't dealt with feeling overwhelmed. Every single one of us knows what it's like to look around at everything we have going on—everything we have to do—and feel like it's just too much.

I've felt this way, and I still do feel this way at times. But let me share with you some things I've learned about feeling overwhelmed and about God's grace and mercy. About the way He can bring peace and strength to our minds and hearts even as we attempt to spin an impossible number of plates all at the same time.

One of the things that help me most when I'm feeling this way is to remember that Jesus understands. How many times do we read in the Bible that crowds were thronging around Jesus? How many times does it say that there were so many people crowding around, all wanting something from Him, that there wasn't even time for Him to eat?

Plenty. Jesus understands what it means to be overwhelmed—to have so much to do that there just isn't enough time in the day to get it all done. He understands dealing with others' demands, the task you were put here on earth to do, and even grief all at the same time.

So the first thing we can do in order to bring abundance to our lives in the midst of feeling—or being—overwhelmed is to remember that Jesus understands, and so do other moms. We're not going through something no one else on this planet has ever gone through. Every mom knows how you're feeling, and Jesus does too.

I know this won't completely take away your feeling of being overwhelmed, but sometimes it helps to stop and remember that others understand and sympathize.

The second thing we can do in the midst of feeling over-whelmed is to do what Jesus did when He was overwhelmed. Check out Matthew 14:22-23. This takes place immediately after Jesus performed a miracle and fed 5,000 men (plus women and chil-dren). He had been preaching all day, and then He performed a miracle so everyone could eat. According to Matthew, this is what happened next:

> Immediately Jesus made the disciples get into the boat and go on ahead of him to the other side, while he dismissed the crowd. After he had dismissed them, he went up on a mountainside by himself to pray. When evening came, he was there alone (*NIV*).

And check out what happened a little earlier, after Jesus was informed that His cousin, John the Baptist, had been murdered:

> When Jesus heard what had happened, he withdrew by boat privately to a solitary place (Matt. 14:13, *NIV*).

Earlier still, when Jesus was faced with the huge task of choosing the men who would be His closest companions, He made that monumental decision this way:

> Jesus went out to a mountainside to pray, and spent the night praying to God (Luke 6:12, *NIV*).

See the trend? When Jesus was overwhelmed with need, when He had an important task to be done, or when He was grieving, He got alone with His Father. Jesus knew, more so than any of us, that abundant life is to be found in the Father, not in earthly circumstances. So His strategy for dealing with life when it was overwhelming—the same strategy that should be ours—was to get alone with God.

"But I don't have time!" you might protest.

It may be true that you don't have enough time to get alone with God for extended periods. But think about it this way: Do you have enough time *not* to get alone with Him? In other words, do you really think you can deal well with the overwhelming circumstances of your life without getting alone with your God?

We've already discussed the fact that you may not have a solid hour (or even a solid 15 minutes) to spend alone with Him. But even the busiest of us can find 5 minutes a day to spend one on One with our heavenly Father—especially when that Father is the only one who can truly help us cope with being overwhelmed.

What do we do when we actually succeed in getting alone with Him? It depends. We might remain silent before Him. We might pour out our hearts. We might sing, dance or draw. The point is that when we get alone with God—when we seek Him for who He is—we will encounter abundant life just by being in His presence.

How does this help us when our quiet time is over, and we have to return to the same circumstances that overwhelmed us in the first place? Put simply, we will return to those circumstances in the company of God, rather than alone. We will have Someone to walk through them with us—Someone who loves us deeply and wants to help us.

We can't adequately handle these feelings on our own. We can't bear our burdens on our own. So when we feel burdened—when we're overwhelmed—why wouldn't we spend a few minutes with God? Why would we struggle alone beneath our load, when abundant life and abundant help are only as far away as reaching out with our hearts?

Jesus promised that He would give us peace in a way that the world, or doing it on our own, cannot give. So when you feel overwhelmed, precious mom, don't hesitate to take advantage of what Jesus is offering. Run to Him. Spend time in His grace and goodness, soaking up abundant life. Ask Him for His help, and you will receive it. Let Him bear your burdens with you.

All this is only as far away as it takes you to reach out.

Comparing Yourself to Others

I spent years of my life comparing myself to others who were prettier than I was (or so I thought, at least) and feeling bad that I came up short.

It's easy to do, isn't it? To compare ourselves to others who are prettier, richer, smarter or more creative than we are and then feel bad about ourselves because we are "less" in those areas.

Maybe another mom's children are better dressed. Maybe they're better behaved. Maybe *she's* better dressed—or prettier. Maybe she has the house or husband or car we wish we had. Maybe she gets to sing solos in church, and we don't.

Whatever the exact nature of the comparison, the point is that we measure ourselves against others—and decide that we are inferior to them because the details of our lives don't match up.

So how can we change our tendency to compare ourselves to others into abundant life? Once again, we get to know God, and He takes care of the change. Let's talk about what that looks like.

First, we have to learn some important things about God and His character. Once we know these things—when we really "get it"—we won't be as tempted to compare ourselves to others—and even if we do, it won't hurt as much. We might even rejoice with other people at the gifts God has given them.

The first thing we have to know about God is that He designed each of us for a purpose. You are not just some random collection of atoms that just happened to result from your earthly mother and father. You were designed carefully and uniquely by God. Look at what God said to the prophet Jeremiah:

Before I formed you in the womb I knew you, before you were born I set you apart (Jer. 1:5, *NIV*).

The same is true for you. Even before you were made, God knew you. He knew you as a person—as the person He was about to create. Did you catch that this verse says, "Before *I* formed you"? God formed you—not your earthly parents, not an accident. God Himself formed you—with intention. Now look at what else Scripture says about you:

I praise you because I am fearfully and wonderfully made; your works are wonderful, I know that full well (Ps. 139:14, *NIV*).

You are "fearfully and wonderfully made." Not "adequately" made, or made in a "mediocre" fashion. You are marvelous! You, as God's work, are wonderful!

Why do we have such trouble believing this? That's a whole book in itself, but suffice it to say this: Somewhere along the line, we've bought into Satan's lie that we're *not* wonderful. That we're not much of anything at all. That everyone else is "more" than we are, and we're "less than."

That's why knowing God is so important if we want to replace comparing ourselves to others with abundant life: We have to know what He says about us. And because He never lies, we know that what He says is absolutely true. We *are* wonderfully made. We *are* His wonderful work. We just have to decide to believe Him rather than Satan's voice that whispers (or shouts) something else into our ear.

As we get to know God better and better, we'll realize something—that He loves us incredibly. Sure, we know this in our heads, but the better we know Him, the more we'll grasp it with our hearts. The mom who's deeply, perfectly loved by God—and knows it—has no need to compare herself with anyone else. It doesn't matter to her if she's more or less than someone else in terms of earthly standards, because God says she's wonderful—and that's what matters to her.

Questioning Ourselves

I told you at the beginning of this book how easy I thought parenting was going to be. I had read books and talked with experts, and I figured it wasn't rocket science anyway, so I was pretty sure that parenting would be a piece of cake.

It wasn't. It was a lot harder than I had thought it would be.

There have been many times since becoming a mom when I questioned myself. What was the right thing to do? Was what I did the best choice? Was I doing well enough as a mom?

At a recent retreat I conducted, I asked the assembled group of moms this question: "How many of you never struggle with wondering whether or not you're doing the right thing, or whether or not you're doing well enough as a mom?" Not a single mom raised her hand.

It's a pretty universal experience, just like feeling overwhelmed and comparing ourselves to others. Given that so many moms struggle with this issue to one extent or another, I want us to take a moment to look at how knowing God better can help us overcome this issue and lead to more abundant life.

But first, we need to look at why we question ourselves. Why we aren't always certain what a good job looks like, or if we're doing one. The first reason is simply that we don't have the amount of wisdom we need in order to do this job called motherhood perfectly.

Not a single one of us knows everything, and we're well aware that we don't know everything. In fact, sometimes we're hyper-aware that we don't know everything. This can lead us to question ourselves. It's like this: We think, *I know I don't know everything, so I wonder what I'm supposed to do,* or, *I don't know if I'm doing this right.*

How can knowing God better help us when we wonder about these things? The answer is simply this: God has promised us wisdom. The apostle James tells us:

> If any of you lacks wisdom, [she] should ask God, who gives generously to all without finding fault, and it will be given to [her] (Jas. 1:5, *NIV*).

James doesn't say that wisdom might be given, or that we can hope that it will be given. Instead, he makes this guarantee: It *will* be given. God *will* give us sufficient wisdom to do our job, and to do it well.

Now what does this have to do with knowing God? Couldn't we just ignore God most of the time and then ask Him for wisdom when we need it?

No. James was writing to a group of Christians who loved God. James presupposed that the people he was talking to loved God and knew Him. That's because God rarely dispenses His wisdom to people who don't care about Him and who only want Him for what He can do for them. Of course, He can give wisdom to anybody He wants, but He's much more likely to speak wisdom into the life of a mom who knows and loves Him—and who seeks His wisdom.

See, that's the thing—you do have to ask. James says that anyone who needs wisdom must ask. We can't expect God to bestow wisdom into our lives without our ever having to ask for it. We need to show Him that we're interested in His wisdom, and one great way to do that is to take to heart the truth that the way to abundant life involves knowing Him, and then to pursue Him.

It's possible that God might not grant us His wisdom the first time we ask for it. Sometimes, He wants us to demonstrate that we truly are interested in hearing what He has to say. Other times, He may choose to wait before dispensing His wisdom for reasons unknown to us. But He *will* do it. He has promised, and He cannot lie.

Another reason we might question ourselves is that others question us. I've spoken with many women who do not have good relationships with their parents and/or in-laws. Many of these women talk about how their parents or their husband's parents question their parenting decisions. Sometimes other family members, or even our friends, may question us. With the important people in our lives questioning what we're doing (or not doing), it can be hard to have confidence in our parenting decisions.

How can knowing God help with that? When we are criticized, we can take those criticisms to Him and ask Him whether or not they're valid. Sometimes we know good and well that the criticisms are invalid. (For example, I was once told that if I simply spanked my son more, he wouldn't have the problems he was having. Those problems had a name, by the way: Asperger's.) Other times, we're not sure. In those times, we can take the issue to God and ask Him to show us whether or not there are things we need to do differently.

It can be hard to go against the counsel of someone close to you. But if God says their criticism is invalid, or if He directs you to go another way, you can do it. Why? Because you know that He knows best; you also know that He's never yet directed you wrong, and He never will.

Dealing with the people who criticize us requires setting firm boundaries. It also requires dealing rightly with them, even if they're not doing so with us. God gives us guidance in this area as well.

He tells us to honor parents and to love others as ourselves. This doesn't mean that we necessarily have to take someone's criticism to heart. It does mean, however, that we need to treat them the way God wants us to. As we do so, perhaps they'll realize that their criticism was invalid. Perhaps they'll see Christ in us. Even if neither of those things happens, at least we may avert an argument by treating others the way God tells us to.

Of course, we can't control the way others respond to us. There may still be an argument if we don't take their advice. But God has given us a way to bring peace into our hearts and minds even when others are criticizing us. If we know Him and run to Him with our questions and feelings about being criticized, He'll tell us the right thing to do and He'll help us deal with those feelings.

It's abundant life even in the midst of criticism.

Abundant Living Action Points

1. Are you feeling overwhelmed? Make plans for a time when you can get alone with God—even if only for five minutes. Also make plans for getting alone with Him for a longer period of time.

2. Do you tend to compare yourself to others? Is there a specific person you compare yourself to? Name that person, and name the area in which you compare yourself. Look up what the Bible has to say about whether or not that area is important.

3. Is there someone in your life who criticizes your parenting? Who is this person? What steps could you take to make peace with this person, at least as far as is possible?

For a more in-depth study of the topics of each chapter, see the Bible study at the end of this book.

Abundance in the Home

*The best way to keep children at home is to make the home atmosphere
pleasant, and let the air out of the tires.*

DOROTHY PARKER

This one's gotta be easy, right? I mean, don't we all have abundance
in our homes?

Abundant dirty dishes.

Abundant loads of laundry.

Abundant chances to referee disputes about things that don't
really matter.

Abundant diapers, trips somewhere in the car, and repeated
explanations.

Yep. All those things are abundant for virtually every mom.

But that's not the kind of abundance we're talking about here.
In this chapter, we're going to explore not just an abundance of
tasks we don't want to do, disputes to referee or messes to clean,
but abundant life in the midst of . . . well, living.

How can a mom find abundant life when her schedule is overbooked and crazy?

How can she find abundant life when her house is a wreck?

Let's talk about both of those things.

Abundant Scheduling

Most of us have abundant scheduling down to a fine art. We're
experts at cramming things into every last bit of our day. We're
overbooked and overscheduled, and we don't see how we could

fit one more thing in. Yet something comes up, and somehow we find a place for it.

True, there will be seasons in life when our schedules are busier than others. There will be times when it's necessary to have a hectic schedule for a period of time. But for most of us, it's not necessary to have a hectic schedule as a way of life.

Having children in the home does lend a certain amount of hecticness even to the most well-organized schedule. There are doctors' appointments to show up for, groceries to shop for, and play dates to arrange. Then there are all the other things we deem absolutely necessary and manage somehow to fit into our schedules.

And this is where we're going to start looking at how to find abundance in the midst of having a chaotic schedule—with our schedules themselves.

Some things, as we have said, are necessary. They simply have to be accomplished. Other things are optional. Yet too often we term nearly everything "necessary" and almost nothing "optional."

Currently, our family's schedule is pretty busy. We have church on Sunday mornings. My husband works Monday through Friday. Two of our kids attend public school, and I school two of them in our home while my husband is at work. Tuesday evenings, Lindsey has gymnastics while my husband and I work out at the Y. Wednesday evenings, we have church. Thursday evenings, we again work out at the Y, and later I serve as the teaching assistant for a biblical Greek class at church. Then there are birthday parties and chores on Saturdays, as well as a final workout and the myriad other things we couldn't get done during the week. Oh, and did I mention that I've been asked to teach an English as a Second Language class on Monday nights?

So I understand having a busy schedule. Really, I do. When the pressure of my schedule gets to me, I have to do the same thing I'm encouraging you to do. I have to stop and examine each item on my schedule and determine which are really, truly necessary at this point in our lives and which could be reduced or eliminated.

Perhaps, like me, you look at your schedule and wonder how you can eliminate anything at all. That's where our relationship with God comes in. That's where knowing Him is helpful, because we can go to Him and ask for His wisdom (there's James 1:5 again!) in knowing what should be part of our lives and what should go by the wayside.

There have been times when God has told me that something was not to be a part of my schedule, even though I wanted to do it. The class I've been asked to teach on Mondays is one such example. He's clearly said, both in my spirit and through my husband, that it would not be good at all for our family life right now. Therefore, I have to say no, even though I would really love doing it.

It's easy to think of all the reasons I would enjoy doing it: I could become even more fluent in Spanish, I would enjoy teaching, I like the people I'd be working with, and so forth. But because I know God, and because I trust Him, I'm going to say no to the class—at least at this point in my life.

You can do that too. Bring each item on your schedule before Him. Ask Him whether or not it truly needs to happen. The only thing is, you have to be willing to hear His answer. If He knows you're not really interested in hearing what He has to say, He might not bother speaking to you in this area at all. He might just let you go on and on in your schedule, becoming more and more stressed and frustrated (which is not abundant life, by the way), until you *are* ready to listen to Him.

On the other hand, if you're willing to eliminate whatever He tells you to eliminate, you will find that you and your family are more at peace without that thing (or those things). That your life is somehow more abundant now that it's less full. I don't know exactly how that works, but I do know that in God's economy, things sometimes work backward, or opposite from the way we'd expect. Clearing your schedule is one of those times. A clear schedule with available open slots can be much more abundant than one that's packed out.

Of course, there will be times when you truly can't or shouldn't eliminate anything from your schedule. This will not be true the majority of the time, but such situations will arise. Listening to God's voice in the area of scheduling doesn't always mean you'll have lots of free time; in fact, sometimes the opposite may be true, and you may have to be very busy for God for a season.

Just make sure you're busy because He wants you to be and not because you've tried to cram too many or the wrong things into your schedule. If that's the case—that your schedule is exactly what He wants it to be for now—then He can still help you experience abundant life even in the midst of the craziness.

We all know that Jesus experienced abundant life, and His schedule was often jam-packed. We also know that He was doing His Father's will. So how did He do it? How did He keep a crazy schedule without going crazy Himself?

First, as we've said, He made sure that He was doing His Father's will. Second, He relied on His Father to get Him through the stressful times. We've already read about some times when Jesus took off by Himself to pray. I've encouraged you to do the same thing, and I hope that you make regular alone-time with God a part of your life.

Jesus knew that without regular spiritual nourishment from His Father, He wouldn't make it spiritually—which is what we're talking about here: making it spiritually through overscheduled times. If *He* needed His Father's strength, how much more do we mere human beings need it?

Receiving God's strength is where knowing God comes in—and it's where abundant life can enter into the midst of even the craziest schedule. If you're like me, many times you try to accomplish things on your own without really thinking about asking God for help. After all, we're supposed to be able to handle our day-to-day lives on our own, right?

Wrong. Somewhere, somehow, we've gotten this idea that we should be able to accomplish the little stuff all by ourselves, and we

should only need God for the really big stuff, like when someone
loses a job or gets cancer. I'm not sure where that idea came from,
except that I bet the devil had everything to do with it. Because
we mere mortals can't possibly make it through life, especially
when life is hectic, with anything less than God's strength.

So how does that work? How do we appropriate God's
strength when we need it? I hope the answer is freeing to you.
It was to me.

The way we appropriate God's strength is, first, to admit
our desperate need of it. After all, strong people don't need
strength. Only weak people need it. So we have to be willing
to admit that we are weak, which most of us don't like to do.
We have to admit that there's a difference between the level
we're at and the place we'd like to be. We have to acknowledge
the fact that we can't do life on our own—that without God to
help us, we're drowning.

It's like when Peter walked on water. Let's review the story:

Immediately Jesus made the disciples get into the boat
and go on ahead of him to the other side, while he dismissed the crowd. After he had dismissed them, he went
up on a mountainside by himself to pray. When evening
came, he was there alone, but the boat was already a con-
siderable distance from land, buffeted by the waves because the wind was against it. During the fourth watch
of the night Jesus went out to them, walking on the
lake. When the disciples saw him walking on the lake,
they were terrified. "It's a ghost," they said, and cried
out in fear. But Jesus immediately said to them: "Take
courage! It is I. Don't be afraid." "Lord, if it's you," Peter
replied, "tell me to come to you on the water." "Come,"
he said. Then Peter got down out of the boat, walked on
the water and came toward Jesus. But when he saw the
wind, he was afraid and, beginning to sink, cried out,

"Lord, save me!" Immediately Jesus reached out his hand and caught him. "You of little faith," he said, "why did you doubt?" (Matt. 14:22-31, *NIV*).

Peter started out strong. He started out focusing on Jesus and miraculously walking on that raging water. But then he took his eyes off of Jesus, and he began to sink. So it is with us. We take our eyes off of Jesus and put them on the details of our lives, and we start to go down.

But take heart, moms, because what Jesus did for Peter, He will do for us too. Peter, realizing that he was drowning, cried out to Jesus to save him. And Jesus did. He didn't let Peter drown. He used His own strength to lift Peter up out of the water.

It wouldn't have been easy for you or for me to stand there on the water and lift a grown man up onto the top of the waves with us. In fact, we couldn't have done it. But for Jesus, it was no problem. That brings up a point we need to take to heart: We may not understand exactly how Jesus grants us His strength, but we don't have to. Our job is to ask for it; His is to provide it.

So cry out to Him, moms. Cry out for His strength. Let Him lift you up out of that water. He may do it instantly, or He may wait for the time He knows is right. But He won't let you drown. This Person whom you love more than anything will reach down to you and lift you up. But you have to humble yourself enough to ask. As James instructs, "Humble yourselves before the Lord, and he will lift you up" (Jas. 4:10, *NIV*).

Abundant Mess

I have to admit that my house isn't the cleanest right now. I've been working on this book during many of the times when I would normally have been cleaning. Around me, I can see and think of things I would like to clean—or have my children clean.

Perhaps this describes your house too. Maybe you'd like it to be a lot neater than it is. Maybe you'd like to be able to find things quickly and easily once in a while. Maybe you'd like for there to be a sense of order to your home.

How can you find abundant life in the midst of a house that's such a wreck you can't seem to find *anything* in it? That's what this section is all about.

If you're hoping that I can tell you how to take care of your kids and keep a spotless home at the same time, you're going to be disappointed. But if you're looking for the way to experience abundant life even when your house doesn't look perfect, that's what you'll find, because I'm going to share with you two things God taught me about living abundantly when the house is a wreck. The first might not surprise you; the second might.

Let's be honest, ladies: Many times the house is a wreck not because it has to be, but because we don't clean it like we should. It's far easier (and more fun) to spend time in leisure pursuits than it is to scrub toilets. But we do have a responsibility to be keepers of our homes, and to give our best effort toward keeping them neat and orderly.

Lest you think I'm just telling you to try harder when you're already trying as hard as you can, let me assure you that that's not the case. I'm talking in this section to those of us who really do need to try harder because we're not making a good-faith effort to do our best.

Sometimes, it's easy to be lazy or to shirk our responsibilities. If this describes you, then you need to confess your sin to God and ask Him to help you put forth a better effort and do a better job. God has made us stewards of our homes, and when we don't do our best to take care of them, we're failing to care for God's gifts. For His resources. For the things that are His, which He has entrusted to us for a time. And then we wonder why we're not at peace about the way our homes look.

But if this doesn't describe you—if you're truly putting forth your best effort, yet your house still doesn't look like you want it to—then the following part of the chapter is for you.

I told you about a time when a friend of mine suggested that I lower my standards. She meant that I shouldn't strive for perfection, but rather for doing my best. Fortunately, that's the exact same thing God wants from us: our best.

That's where knowing God helps you experience abundant life: He will help you know exactly how much you should accomplish; He will help you do it; and then He will help you be content with the results.

Maybe one day, God wants you to spend extra time playing with your children instead of cleaning. I've heard older women say they wished they'd spent more time with their kids when the kids were young, but I have never heard a woman say she wished she had spent less time with her children and more time cleaning.

Maybe God wants you to minister to a hurting friend instead of getting the kitchen sparkling clean.

Maybe He wants you to spend extra time with Him in prayer instead of vacuuming.

Maybe He has something else in mind for you to do instead of getting your house spic-and-span. The wise woman who knows God will listen to His voice and do the things He suggests, even if they aren't what she thought He would want.

In this situation, leaving a chore undone doesn't have to result in the usual nagging annoyance that it's not done. You see, knowing God also means that He can teach you to be content, whatever your circumstances. Usually this teaching involves lots of opportunities to practice being content in less-than-desirable circumstances, but only if He knows that's what it will take.

When you've done your best, and both you and God know it, He can grant you contentment with the results, whatever they are. This doesn't necessarily mean you'll be jumping up and down for joy, but you can be content. You know you can live with your circumstances. You can have peace in your heart and mind despite them.

In other words, if you've done your best, you can live abundantly in your heart and mind, no matter the busyness of your schedule or the state of your home.

Abundant Living Action Steps

1. Look at your schedule. Is there anything you need to eliminate or reduce? Pray over each item, asking God whether it's really necessary for your family.
2. Do you do your best to clean? If so, thank God for the state of your home, because it reflects His plan for your life. If not, ask Him what you legitimately need to take on in order to be doing your best.

For a more in-depth study of the topics of each chapter, see the Bible study at the end of this book.

Abundance in Relationships

*The great motherhood friendships are the ones in which two women
can admit [how difficult mothering is] quietly to each other,
over cups of tea at a table sticky with spilled apple juice and
littered with markers without tops.*

ANNA QUINDLEN

One afternoon, several years ago, my husband and I found ourselves alone. The kids were all taking naps. The house was neat and
quiet. We had time to ourselves to do anything we wanted to do.

"The kids are all in bed," my husband pointed out.

"Yeah," I said. "Finally."

"Nobody to bother us," Phil said.

"True," I agreed.

We looked at each other. "Let's take a nap," we sighed together.
And we did.

It's hard to have abundant time alone with your husband when
you're in the midst of parenting. For that matter, it's hard to have
abundant time alone with anyone, including family and friends
as well as each of your children individually (assuming you have
more than one).

How, then, can we have abundant relationships in the midst
of the messiness of mothering? Fortunately, there are several ways,
and that's what we'll look at in this chapter. We'll also look at how
to have abundance in relationships even when those relationships
aren't good. And of course we'll look at what knowing God, the
Source of abundant life, has to do with all of this.

Your Relationship with Your Husband

If you're married, your relationship with your husband is supposed to be your most important earthly relationship, surpassing even your relationships with your children. But often, in the messiness of motherhood, it gets pushed aside. Into the background maybe. After all, the children are so needy. They can't dress themselves, feed themselves, or change their own diapers. Or maybe they're a little older and are better able to fend for themselves, but they can't drive themselves back and forth to all their activities. Or maybe they can drive, but even then, they still need you. As we've seen, a mom's relationship to her children is a relationship like no other.

How, then, do you keep your relationship with your husband primary when the younger people in your life are clamoring for your attention?

It's hard. Believe me, I know it is. But it's doable. Even in the midst of mothering.

The first thing we can do to keep this most important earthly relationship primary is to realize that it's supposed to be primary. Scripture tells us that husband and wife "shall become one flesh" (Gen. 2:24), something it doesn't even say about our children. We and our husbands are supposed to be two sides of the same coin. Different, yes, but one coin.

Fortunately, the New Testament gives us more detail about what this relationship is supposed to look like:

> Wives, submit to your husbands as to the Lord. For the husband is the head of the wife as Christ is the head of the church, his body, of which he is the Savior. Now as the church submits to Christ, so also wives should submit to their husbands in everything. Husbands, love your wives, just as Christ loved the church and gave himself up for her to make her holy, cleansing her by the washing with water through the word, and to present her to himself as a radiant church, without stain or wrinkle or any other blemish, but

holy and blameless. In this same way, husbands ought to love their wives as their own bodies. He who loves his wife loves himself. After all, no one ever hated his own body, but he feeds and cares for it, just as Christ does the church—for we are members of his body. "For this reason a man will leave his father and mother and be united to his wife, and the two will become one flesh." This is a profound mystery—but I am talking about Christ and the church. However, each one of you also must love his wife as he loves himself, and the wife must respect her husband (Eph. 5:22-33, *NIV*).

We are to make every effort to make sure our marriages look like this. In other words, we are to do our part—submitting to our husbands and allowing them to be leaders, and respecting them. Elsewhere in Scripture, we as believers are told to clothe ourselves with humility toward one another (see 1 Pet. 5:5) and to honor one another above ourselves (see Rom. 12:10). Putting all these things together, we need to be treating our husbands like they are pretty special people.

That's where it gets difficult. How do we find time to do that while we're busy with the kids?

The answer is this: We may not always have time to spend alone with our husbands (though if it's important to us, we'll make time), but we can always—no matter how much time we have—honor and prefer our husbands above ourselves.

Most of us spend far more time thinking about how our husbands can or should meet our needs than we do about how we can meet their needs. We spend more time focusing on the things our husbands don't do in terms of making us feel special than we do on the things *we* could do that would make *them* feel special.

If we want to have abundance in our relationships with our husbands, we need to flip our thinking around. Instead of focusing on what they need to be doing, we should focus on ourselves. Instead of dwelling on how they should treat us, we ought to think more about what we can do for them.

A marriage where the wife is primarily concerned with herself and her own needs is not going to be nearly as satisfying as a marriage where the wife puts her husband first. There's freedom in not having to be number one and allowing someone else to hold that treasured position.

I'm not saying that there are never times when it's appropriate for you to ask your husband to meet your needs differently. I'm simply saying that putting him first instead of yourself will lead to the joy and abundant life that Jesus promised.

How can I be so sure? Because it's God's way, and God's way is always right. Whenever we turn aside from how God intended things to be and begin to conduct our relationships in our own way, they're not going to feel abundant to us. They're going to feel small and narrow. Constricted. Yet when we give up our right to be primary in the relationship, we somehow gain rather than lose. Remember how we said that sometimes God's economy works backward? This is one of those times.

So yes, plan date nights with your husband. Get a babysitter when you can so that you can have some alone time. But if you want an abundant relationship with your husband, you can have one simply by following God's design for your relationship, whether you have frequent date nights or not.

Of course, it takes two people to make this really work. You may be the only one trying, or at least the one doing most of the trying. If you're in an abusive relationship, you may even have to separate from your husband to keep yourself and your children safe. We'll talk later on in this chapter about doing the best you can do when your efforts aren't equally matched.

But for now, let's move on to how to have abundant relationships with your children.

Abundant Relationships with Your Children

I decided one day that I was going to count Timmy's tantrums. But they were so frequent that I lost count. Was that abundant life?

Then there were all the days when the bickering seemed constant, and I felt like all I did was referee disputes about things that didn't really matter. Was *that* abundant life?

No . . . and yes.

You see, as we've already discussed, abundant life doesn't consist in the perfection of a mom's circumstances. It's possible to have abundant relationships with your children even when those relationships aren't perfect. In this section we'll talk about how.

Fortunately, God in His wisdom has once again given us insight into what relationships between parents and children should look like. Paul puts it this way:

And, ye fathers, provoke not your children to wrath: but bring them up in the nurture and admonition of the Lord (Eph. 6:4, *KJV*).

Many times, we as parents want to focus on the "honor your father and mother" part of God's instruction for this relationship, while ignoring the part about how we're not supposed to provoke our children. Yes, absolutely yes, children need to be taught to honor their parents. This is part of making the parent-child relationship work the way God designed it. But we also need to make sure we're not needlessly causing our children to become bitter or angry.

Do we treat our children kindly? Do we speak to them as gently or politely as we would speak to an adult stranger? Do we treat them with respect, just as we want to be treated? If not, we may be provoking them needlessly and making it harder for them to honor us, which will make the parent-child relationship worse.

Treat my children with respect? Aren't they *supposed to treat* me *with respect?* Certainly they are. But our children are human beings too, deserving of the same respect due to any human being—especially those we claim to love passionately.

So the first step in making sure our relationships with our children are abundant is to make sure we're treating them right instead of provoking them. True, our children won't always like what we have to say. I'm not suggesting that we never say anything that makes our children angry. I'm simply suggesting that if we do, we make sure it's carefully considered and really necessary to be said, instead of being needlessly provoking. That's abundance, even when life gets messy.

Another way to promote abundance between you and your children is to express your love in the ways your children can best receive it, and to make it a point to do so. Some children enjoy hearing about your love for them in words; some like seeing it in action; some feel loved when they receive gifts. Have you studied your children enough to know what makes them feel loved?

My son Kenny feels especially loved when I speak uplifting words to him. Of course he likes gifts too, but words are what make him feel most loved. So I try to make it a point to praise him and tell him how hard-working he is, or how handsome or strong, or how much I appreciate something he's done (or refrained from doing).

My daughter Lindsey's love language is quality time. She loves getting alone time with Mama. So I make sure that we get time together every so often, just her and me. When we're alone together, we go do something she considers fun (which is usually something I consider fun too, because we're a lot alike in that department). I tell her how much I'm enjoying spending time with her, and she grins and tells me the same. Sometimes she just grins, full of contentment and joy.

I love these two children equally, but I show them love in different ways. If I spent more alone time with Kenny, he would enjoy it, but he wouldn't feel as loved as if I made sure to tell him what a great boy he is and how blessed I am to have him. Likewise, Lindsey enjoys hearing me verbally express my thanks or appreciation for something she's done, but she feels even more loved when I spend time with her. So one way I try to make my relationships with Kenny and Lindsey (and my other children) abundant is to be proactive about expressing my love, and to do so in the way that child will best receive it.

Yes, your children will still disobey at times. Yes, they will bicker. Yes, they will do things wrong and have to be corrected. Yes, you will still have to change tons of diapers and drive to thousands of activities. And yes, your relationship with your children may still be difficult.

But you can make life as abundant as possible in the midst of all those things if you treat your children right by pouring out love upon them and not provoking them, and by frequently expressing your love in the way they long to receive it.

Abundant Relationships with Friends and Family

I'll admit that when I first thought about writing this section, I wasn't sure what I would say. How can you have abundant relationships with friends and family when there's no time to be together? I mean, we're busy moms. We sometimes don't have time to take a shower or cook a nice meal, much less spend a few hours (or longer) with a girlfriend. How in the world can we have abundant relationships with friends and family members when we're so busy as moms?

It's hard to make time to spend with our loved ones, I know. Believe me, I know. I'd love to have more time to spend with them than I do, but that simply isn't possible right now. So how do I—how do you—have abundant relationships when there simply isn't as much time as we would like?

Once again, knowing God and His ways will help us find the answer.

First, it's important to remember that God commands us not to forsake assembling together in worship:

Not forsaking the assembling of ourselves together, as the manner of some is; but exhorting one another: and so much the more, as ye see the day approaching (Heb. 10:25, *KJV*).

This verse brings up two good points that are going to provide our answer. In the original context, this verse is speaking to Christians and commanding them not to stop meeting for worship. Often, many of our friendships will be with people we know from church, or at least other believers. If we forsake meeting together—if we don't bother to go to church ever—we'll miss out not only on the chance to worship God in community, along with all the benefits that brings, but also on a prime opportunity to bond with like-minded people who may become close friends, or at least a source of support for us in times of trouble.

I believe this verse also applies to us as moms, not just as Christians. We're not to give up trying to meet with our friends and family. We do indeed need to take what time we have available and use it for bonding, fun and fellowship. If we stop trying, we miss out.

If we're too busy ever to find time for our friends, we're probably too busy. Could we really not meet with a close friend once a month? It doesn't have to cost anything, so money is no excuse. It could be over the telephone, which makes things even more convenient (though face-to-face time is necessary sometimes too). But if we almost never have time for our friends, we're forsaking the fellowship we could be having.

In this day of Facebook and texting and email, staying in touch with friends is easier than ever. I have a dear friend—a "heart friend," as she puts it—who is a missionary in Africa, and we are still able to stay in touch (when she's in a region that permits Internet contact), even from opposite sides of the world.

I also have a friend Lori, whom I've mentioned before, who has five kids approximately the same ages as mine. She and I don't get to spend as much face-time together as we would like—at least not without children in tow—but we do what we can, and we text or call or send messages via Facebook when we're able. That way, we can stay in contact several times per week.

You can think of creative ways to stay in touch too. Maybe you have time to go out to dinner with your friend, your sister or your mom. Maybe you don't, but you have 30 seconds to send a text. Maybe you have time to write that email. If you have time to spend on Facebook or playing online games, you have time to contact a loved one and spend at least some virtual time together. If you can't connect right away, you can always reach out to her and then wait for her to respond when she is able.

The second part of this verse gives us another important idea. When we are with our friends and family, we need to be exhorting one another. We need to be building one another up. The apostle Paul gives us this instruction:

> Do not let any unwholesome talk come out of your mouths, but only what is helpful for building others up according to their needs, that it may benefit those who listen (Eph. 4:29, *NIV*).

Not only should we refrain from unwholesome talk, but we also must make it a point to encourage one another. One way to experience abundant life is to spend our time together encouraging one another and building one another up.

Best friends know each other intimately. Family members often do too. Who better to build each other up than people who know each other so well? You are uniquely situated to speak encouragement into a sister's life (whether a biological or a spiritual sister) because you know her so well, and she is in the same position to speak encouragement into yours.

Why did God make it a point to command us to encourage one another? Because He knows how we feel both when we're encouraged and when we're the ones doing the encouraging. Either way, we feel built up, strengthened and uplifted. We feel more able to face whatever might come our way. We're more at peace.

Peace, strength and encouragement. These are all elements of abundant life. So when we make it a point to stay in contact with one another as much as we can, and when we spend our time together encouraging one another, we find out more of what abundant life is all about.

Even Jesus Himself had friends and family around Him when He walked this earth. He knows how important that kind of fellowship is. He wants it for you too. He wants you to be able to experience this type of abundant life.

But What If . . . ?

What if your relationship with your husband isn't good? What if he doesn't do his part in meeting your needs? What if you're on the verge of a divorce?

What if your children tell you they hate you? What if they simply don't respect you? What if life with them is almost always hard?

And what if you don't have a close friend right now on whom you can count? What if you can't rely on your family either, because the relationships aren't good, and may have never been?

What then? What does abundance look like then?

It's a hard and painful question to consider. One of the answers may at first seem painful too.

That answer is this: God sometimes allows relationships to be difficult because He wants to show us exactly how we need to be more like Christ.

Not that He ever causes people to sin against us or causes relationships to be needlessly difficult—far from it. But He does sometimes allow sin and difficulties, and one reason He does is to point out to us the ways in which we are not yet as conformed to the character of Christ as He wants us to be.

So the first step in experiencing abundance through difficult relationships is to realize that they have the potential to draw us closer to Christ.

I've written elsewhere that my relationships with my parents are difficult. I would not choose for this to be the case—in fact, quite the opposite. I long for these relationships to be what everyone wants from relationships with her parents. But I must also recognize that through these difficult relationships, I have learned a lot about my Christlikeness—or lack thereof.

You see, I'm not perfect either. Forgiveness is a struggle for me, and I don't always forgive perfectly. Each time an offense occurs, I'm tempted to go over and over it in my mind, rehearsing how I'm right and they're wrong. But that's not what Christ would do. Nor is it what He wants me to do. So each time I have trouble forgiving, God reminds me that I need to be more like His Son, Christ, who, as He was being *crucified*, prayed for God to forgive His tormentors.

Perhaps your struggle isn't with forgiveness. Perhaps it's with responding rightly when someone sins against you. (I have trouble with that one too sometimes.) When your husband fails to meet your needs, when your family member says something hurtful, or when your children tell you that they hate you, perhaps your temptation is to lash out against them in the same way.

Christ, however, never did this. Even when the Jews were accusing Him of many things prior to His crucifixion, He didn't do it. Check out this example:

> When the leading priests and other leaders made their accusations against him, Jesus remained silent. "Don't you hear their many charges against you?" Pilate demanded. But Jesus said nothing, much to the governor's great surprise (Matt. 27:12-14, *NLT*).

Pilate had presided over hundreds or perhaps thousands of trials and crucifixions. He was shocked that Jesus wasn't returning insult for insult or even saying anything at all in response to those who were mistreating Him.

I'm not saying you should never say anything when someone mistreats you. Even Jesus responded strongly when it was appropriate—for example, in dealing with the moneychangers at the Temple (see Matt. 21:12-13). There are times when you most certainly should speak up. But you should never respond by engaging in the same kind of sinful behavior that someone else is inflicting on you. Jesus didn't, and He doesn't want you to either.

You can probably think of many other ways in which difficult relationships reveal how we're not like Christ. Maybe they show us that we're not patient, loving or kind. Maybe they show us that we are deceitful or manipulative. Whatever the case, the fact is that they point out the areas in which we are most unlike Jesus and most need to grow.

They also help us get to know Jesus better. That's because not only do difficult relationships show us where we need to be more like Jesus, but they also prompt us to pray more. When we do that, we get to know God better as we talk with Him and listen to Him.

So if difficult relationships in my life show me how I can be more like Christ, I rejoice in that. And if they show me how I can know Him better, through prayer over the situation and through studying what He says about how I should respond, then I welcome that.

No, I don't want my relationships to be difficult, and I know you don't want yours to be either. But don't forget that even the most difficult relationships can be doorways to abundant life, if we will just let them be.

Abundant Living Action Points

1. Do you put your husband first? If not, ask God to forgive you and show you how to do so. Then ask your husband to forgive you. And get ready for that abundant life!

2. Do you tend to provoke your children needlessly? Ask God to show you the truth. Then make amends with any child you have hurt in this way.

3. Is there a relationship in your life that's difficult? Take it before God. Thank Him for all the ways this relationship shows you how to be like Jesus and draws you closer to Him.

For a more in-depth study of the topics of each chapter, see the Bible study at the end of this book.

A Final Word

Would you ever have thought that abundant life would look like what we've talked about in these pages? That it's really no more—and no less—than knowing God and finding in Him the ultimate Source of all life?

As you've read through this book, you've heard a lot about what abundant life looks like. You've taken some action steps to begin living more abundantly. Perhaps you have even done the Bible study so that you could dig a little deeper into the concepts presented here.

But now it's time for the rubber to meet the road. Now you're about to put this book down and go back to your life, where nothing has changed.

Except you.

I hope that as you've read this book, God has reached down into your heart and changed it. I hope He's shown you that He is the source of all the abundance you could ever want in your life, and that apart from Him, you're chasing meaningless vanity (see the book of Ecclesiastes). I hope you believe it.

I hope you're also ready to live it.

May I pray for you before we go?

Precious Father God, bless and keep the precious mom who has read these words. Who has heard You speaking to her heart. Who wants to be different and make a difference. Who wants to experience more of that abundant life Your Son promised us. Bless her, God, with the knowledge of You. For only in You is truly abundant life to be found. Give her strength to stand when she's tempted to slip back into old patterns of seeking abundant life elsewhere, or demanding it from others. By Your grace alone, oh Lord, will she make it. Cover her and enfold her in that grace just as she would wrap a blanket around a shivering child. Be ever near to her, and so draw her nearer to You, the Source of all abundant life. In Jesus' name. Amen.

I'll keep praying for you, precious mom. I'll pray that the eyes of your heart continue to be opened to God's presence and the abundant life that He is.

And I'll pray that you'll be able to say along with me, "I knew a lot more about parenting before I had children. But I know a lot more now about abundant life."

chaotic
JOY

Bible Study

Chapter 1—Burden or Blessing?

1. What did you think motherhood was going to be like before you became a mom? Can you identify with any of the unrealistic expectations mentioned in this chapter?
2. How have you been disillusioned as a mom? Can you think of any particular experiences?
3. What is the most difficult aspect of motherhood for you? Why?
4. Do you struggle with feeling like your life is less than abundant? What makes you feel this way?
5. Some parts of motherhood are fantastic. Can you think of any?
6. Read John 10:10. What does it mean to have abundant life in the midst of motherhood?
7. Do you experience any of the four roadblocks to abundance listed here? Which ones?
8. Does your gaze tend to get stuck in the mundane details of motherhood? What does God say should be our primary focus? How could you learn to focus on Him rather than focusing on laundry or dirty dishes?
9. Do you tend to look to perfect circumstances to fulfill your need for abundant life? Circumstances never can be perfect—at least, not for long. How does that make you feel?
10. What gift from God is mentioned in this chapter as the only gift that can truly fulfill the deepest longings of our souls? Do you agree?
11. What would it look like in your life if you were to pursue knowing God? How would your life be different?

Chapter 2—Mommy? Mommy??

1. How does being a parent help you know more about God as your heavenly Father?
2. How does it make you feel to realize that God loves you with the same love with which you love your children, times a billion?
3. What does the fatherhood of God mean to you? How is your understanding of God as Father affected by the earthly father you have or had?

4. Read Matthew 7:11. What does it mean to you that God knows even better than you do how to give good things?

5. Consider the statement: "Being perfectly loved sure sounds like abundant life to me!" Do you agree?

6. What does it mean to you to know that God's love for you is based on your identity, not on anything you have done or failed to do?

7. Read Numbers 23:19. How do you feel knowing that God's love for you is permanent?

8. How does God feel about giving you things? Are you surprised to know this?

9. Did you know that God cares about what happens to you, whether big things or small things? How does this make you feel?

Chapter 3—Someone to Talk To

1. How have your devotional times changed from before you were a mom? Are they more frequent now, or less?

2. Do you experience frustration in trying to make a quiet time happen? What kinds of things have you done in order to try to have a regular devotional time?

3. Does it surprise you to know that God doesn't expect your post-children quiet times to look exactly the same as they did pre-children? What do you think He expects from you in this area now?

4. What is God's ultimate desire for us? How does He accomplish this?

5. Consider this quotation: "It took not having an hour with Him to realize that I had all day with Him." Have you ever thought about it this way?

6. What constitutes acceptable prayer? Do you pray this way?

7. Are you a "seize the moment" kind of person in terms of quiet time, or do you like to have a planned time? How would it change your devotional life to become more of a "seize the moment" person?

8. Consider this statement: "There is marvelous freedom in how you relate to God. You are different from every other person God ever has made or ever will make, so your relationship with Him will be different from any other." What does this mean to you?

9. Read Luke 10:27. Does it simplify your life to know this?

Chapter 4—Sacrifice? Check!

1. What kinds of things have you been called to sacrifice recently for the sake of your children?
2. What is the hardest thing for you to sacrifice as a mom?
3. It's possible to turn sacrifices into fasts and acts of worship. How would things be different if you were to do that? How would you do it?
4. How can fasting help you grow closer to God?
5. Have you ever thought about all the things Jesus sacrificed (not just when He sacrificed His life on the cross)? How does it feel to know that He has sacrificed many of the same things you have?
6. Knowing that Jesus sacrificed many of the things you have sacrificed can make it easier to identify with Him. How does identifying with Him help you draw close to Him?
7. Read Mark 8:35. What would applying this verse look like in your life?

Chapter 5—Say What?

1. Reread the quotation at the beginning of the chapter. Could this be said of you?
2. Teaching children to listen involves teaching them to do what two things? Are you good at listening to God this way?
3. Do you hear God all day long? If not, why do you think that is? If so, what difference does it make in your life?
4. How can you learn to listen to God all day long? Are there any voices you need to silence so that you can hear God?
5. Read 2 Corinthians 10:5. Do you tend to let your feelings control you? Why is this dangerous?
6. Do you hear God speaking to you through your children? How might you learn to hear Him speaking to you this way?
7. Do you hear God when He tries to correct you? Does He ever do this through your children?

8. How does it make you feel to know that God is not just ready and willing but also eager to talk to you all day long? Do you ever take Him up on that?

Chapter 6—Knowing God Through Worship

1. Consider this statement: "That kind of reaction—where we're practically breathless in the face of God's amazing majesty—is truly worshiping God." What other kinds of reactions might you have when you are truly worshiping?
2. Do you connect spirit to Spirit with God on a regular basis through worship? If so, when and how? If not, when was the last time you did?
3. Read Psalm 51:17. What is true worship? What is it not?
4. In order to worship God as busy moms, it's important to learn to connect with Him and worship Him in the midst of the busyness that surrounds us. Do you agree?
5. What are some ways you could connect with God in the midst of all the things going on in your life? Do any of the ways suggested in this chapter particularly jump out at you?
6. Read Matthew 25:31-46. What does it mean to you to know that whenever you do something for someone else, Jesus receives your service as personally done unto Him?
7. Does praying throughout the day come naturally to you? What difference might it make if you learned to pray "continually"?
8. How do you cultivate an attitude of listening to God? What about praising Him?

Chapter 7—Shhhhhhh

1. Does the idea of getting to know God through silence sound like an impossible dream in your household? Does it sound valuable to you?
2. Read Psalm 46:10. Did you ever realize that "being still" before God is a command?

3. What are three voices we might need to silence if we want to hear from God? Do you need to silence (or at least reduce) any of those?

4. One suggestion made in this chapter is to teach our children to be silent at times so that we can spend time listening to God. Does this sound possible? Does it sound like the right thing to do?

5. What are the benefits of being silent before God? How can we learn to do this?

6. Will God speak to us every time we're silent before Him? If not, then what's the point of silence?

7. What does it show God when we're willing to be silent before Him? How do you think this makes Him feel?

Chapter 8—Giving

1. Read Matthew 10:1-8. What had Jesus given the disciples that He commanded them to give freely? What has He given you that He wants you to freely give?

2. What do we need to freely receive from God first and foremost? What does it mean to be saved?

3. Did you know that God delights in meeting your needs? Think of a recent time when you were glad to meet a need of your child's. How much more glad is God to meet your needs?

4. Do you ever get burned out from giving? What can you do when this happens?

5. How are luxuries defined in this chapter? What luxuries do you have in your life that God has provided?

6. To which three people or groups of people do we need to give? How can we decide to whom, when and what to give?

7. How does giving cause us to draw closer to God? What does it have to do with abundant life?

Chapter 9—Frugality

1. Is frugality a positive or negative concept for you? Why?

2. How is frugality defined in this chapter? Do you agree with this definition?
3. Is living within your means easy or difficult for you? Why and how?
4. Consider this statement: "We would never tell God directly that we feel like He hasn't provided enough, but our actions and spending habits show that that's what we believe." Does this describe you?
5. When we're willing to live within our means, what does this show God and a watching world?
6. Read Luke 12:29-31,34. Where is your treasure?
7. How does it make you feel to know that God has promised He will provide for you? Does it ever seem as if He's not fulfilling His promise?
8. What three things will happen if a family lives within their means?
9. Consider this statement: "God sometimes asks us to do without so that He can teach us to rely on Him instead of on our own resources." Do you agree?
10. How can living within your means bless others financially? Can you think of a time when you blessed someone else materially, whether with money or with giving an item? How did being able to do that make you feel?

Chapter 10—Fellowship
1. Does your church host regular fellowships of some kind? Why are these valuable to a church body?
2. What does true Christian fellowship involve? Why is this important?
3. Is the idea of being intimately known scary to you? What benefits might it bring you?
4. Are you part of a group whose members know one another intimately? If so, what advantages does this bring you? If not, where might you find such a group?

5. Why is it important to know and be intimately known?
6. According to this chapter, another reason we need the Body of Christ is to stand by one another in times of trial. Can you recall a time when you stood by another person or someone stood by you in a time of trial?
7. Rebuking one another is hard. Have you ever had to rebuke someone? Have you ever been rebuked? Either way, was it done in a loving manner?
8. In what ways do you make Christian fellowship a priority? Do you believe it's important to do so? Why or why not? What Bible verses can help you answer these questions?
9. How might you find or make time for Christian fellowship?

Chapter 11—Beyond All We Ask or Imagine

1. What is the greatest gift you can imagine receiving?
2. Read Ephesians 3:20-21. How does it make you feel to know that God can do abundantly more than all you ask or imagine?
3. Consider this statement: "It's unbelievable that God would choose to bless us sinners abundantly—to lavish upon us every spiritual blessing without holding some back as consequences for all our sins. Yet that's exactly what He's chosen to do. *Every* spiritual blessing, to an extent that's *abundantly more than we can ask or imagine.*" Why has God chosen to do this? Are you overwhelmed by this knowledge?
4. God not only allows us to know Him, but He also pours blessings into our lives. What are some of the blessings He offers to each of us?
5. What are the fruit of the Spirit? How does God produce them in our lives?
6. What does it mean to grieve the Holy Spirit? How do we sometimes do that?
7. Is it easy or difficult for you to believe that God loves you? Why? Do you agree that you can make a choice of your will to start believing it even if your feelings tell you otherwise?

Chapter 12—Abundant Love

1. How would you define love? Does it necessarily have anything to do with warm, fluffy feelings?
2. Is it easy or difficult for you to love someone else more than you love yourself? What if that person is your child?
3. Can you think of times when your children expressed love to you? What specific incidents do you still remember to this day?
4. What are some everyday, ordinary ways your children have loved you recently?
5. Have you experienced this love for others who love your children? Perhaps for a spouse, grandparents or friends? Why do you think this love happens?
6. Have you ever thought about the love God has for you simply because you love His children? How does understanding your love for the people you listed in Question #5 help you better understand God's love for you?
7. Read John 13:34. What does knowing that these were some of Jesus' last words to His disciples tell you about how important this command was to Him? Why do you think it was so important?

Chapter 13—Abundant Peace

1. How would you complete the sentence "There is peace in our house when . . ."? Do you have this kind of peace often?
2. According to this chapter, it's possible to be at peace all the time. Do you agree? If so, what do you think that means?
3. Read John 14:27. Jesus told His disciples that peace was possible, even in the midst of what they were about to endure. How do you feel, knowing that He says the same thing to you today?
4. What kind of peace does Jesus give?
5. What does it mean that Jesus doesn't give peace as the world gives? How does the world give peace? What is the difference between how Jesus gives and how the world gives?
6. What do we have to do if we want to have peace? Is this easy or difficult for you?

7. Are you good at bringing peace to family members? What could you do to make your home more peaceful in this way?

8. Are there things in your schedule that you need to eliminate or reduce? How would your home be more peaceful if you did so?

9. According to this chapter, what is the most valuable way you can bring peace to your family? Have you done this?

10. What are some other things you can do to bring peace to your family?

11. What are some ways you can bring peace to your physical home?

Chapter 14—Abundant Joy

1. Reread the quotation at the beginning of the chapter. Do you agree?

2. Is it easier for you to focus on the negative or the positive? Why do you think that is?

3. When circumstances bring you joy, do you celebrate? Do you thank God for the blessings He has given you?

4. This chapter talks about a deeper kind of joy that moms experience. Can you think of a time recently when you experienced this deeper joy?

5. Consider this statement: "It's simply not possible to know God in a genuine way yet have a spirit that is less than joyful on a consistent basis. Or put another way, to the extent that we know God, our spirits will be joyful." Do you agree?

6. Can you think of someone who's fun to be around because he or she is so joyful? Are you a person like this?

7. Do you have family and/or friends who bring joy to your heart? Do you have family members who are difficult? How do you prevent these people from stealing your joy?

8. What kinds of things do you like to do when you have the chance to do something relaxing or fun? If you had an hour to yourself right now, what would you do with it? How could you work this activity into your schedule in the near future?

9. Are you generally a negative person or a positive person? Is it possible that your attitude is part of the reason your joy isn't as full as it could be? Read Psalm 51:6 and ask God to show you the truth.

Chapter 15—Abundant Strength

1. What kinds of pressures are you under right now? What about on a regular basis?
2. Do you tend to struggle more with internal or external pressures? Which seem to be stressing you out more?
3. How do you deal with pressure—whether internal, external or both? Do you explode, shut down, or respond in some other way?
4. What does it mean to take a burden to God? How do we do that?
5. It's not always easy to determine whether or not the pressure on us is legitimate. How can we do so accurately?
6. According to this chapter, sometimes it's necessary to lower our standards. What do you think this means? Do you agree? Why or why not?
7. Consider this statement: "When we allow someone else to place a command upon us that God does not want us to follow, we put that person in the position of God. We begin to worship that other person's will instead of God's will. That's idolatry!" Do you agree?
8. Read Psalm 73:26. Do you ever feel like this? What difference would it make if you were to seek God and His strength during these times?
9. Do you cry out to God for strength when you need it? Remember that even if you don't understand exactly how He does it, He can still give you the strength you need to keep going.

Chapter 16—Become Last

1. Consider this quotation: "You'll know whether or not you truly have a servant heart by your reaction to being treated like a servant." Do you agree? Why or why not?

2. What does it mean to have a servant's heart? Do you think you generally have one?

3. Is having a servant's heart difficult or easy for you? Why do you think that's the case?

4. What does having a servant's heart have to do with abundant life?

5. What three rights do we have to give up in order to be true servants? Which right do you find the most difficult to give up?

6. Have you ever thought about the fact that if you are serving, it means your body is healthy enough for you to be able to serve? Would it make a difference in your attitude if you thanked God for your healthy body that allows you the ability to serve?

7. Read Matthew 16:25. What does this have to do with being a servant? What is the reward for being a servant?

Chapter 17—See Your Children as Blessings

1. Is it easier for you to focus on the things your children do wrong and the ways they annoy you, or on the things they do right and the ways they bless you?

2. Consider this statement: "Yet too often we look to circumstances to determine whether or not we feel blessed by our children. Some days we do; some days we don't. We give circumstances a higher authority than we give God's Word in establishing what is and is not a blessing." Are you ever guilty of this?

3. How does it feel to know that God loves you like crazy, no matter what you do or fail to do?

4. Can you think of some things your children have done recently that have really blessed you?

5. Who are some of the people you probably never would have met if you didn't have children? Have you ever thanked God for these blessings?

6. Have you ever thought about the fact that it's a privilege to be a mother at all? Have you, or have any of your friends, experienced infertility, a failed adoption or pregnancy/infant/child

loss? How can you offer comfort or encouragement to someone who is experiencing this kind of grief? If the person is you,
what kind of comfort can you ask God to offer you?

Chapter 18—Come Alongside Others

1. What was your reaction to the story about the preschool stu-
   dent's mother who was making the best of a bad situation? Do
   you think you would have responded to that mom competitively?
2. What are some of the ways moms compete with one another?
   Do you compete with other moms in any of these ways?
3. Do you ever find yourself gossiping about other moms behind
   their backs, or tearing them down when they're not around to
   hear it? What do you think God would say about this?
4. Does it matter to you to know that you are part of a worldwide
   community of moms? Why or why not?
5. Have your experiences with other moms generally been uplifting and helpful, or negative? What do you think others would
   say about their experiences with you?
6. According to this chapter, other moms understand us and can
   help us in ways that those who aren't mothers may not be able
   to. Do you agree? Is this perspective valuable to you?
7. Read the story of Rachel and Leah in Genesis 29 and 30. How
   might things have been different if these moms had realized
   that they were in community, not competition?

Chapter 19—Abundance in the Mind and Heart

1. Do you agree that abundant living comes from knowing God?
2. Do you ever wonder what abundant living looks like in the
   midst of your circumstances? What circumstances make your
   life feel less than abundant? How is God present with you in
   those circumstances?
3. When you feel overwhelmed, do you tend to try to solve it
   yourself, or do you take it to God? Do you ever get alone with
   Him and just seek Him for Himself?

4. What does it mean to you to know that Jesus sympathizes with you when you feel overwhelmed?

5. Do you tend to compare yourself to others? In what areas? Is there a specific person to whom you tend to compare yourself? Who is she or he?

6. How can knowing God help you stop comparing yourself to others? Do you think it really works this way?

7. Read Psalm 139:14. Do you believe this applies to you? What difference does this make in your life, or what difference would it make if you more fully believed it?

8. Do you tend to question yourself, or are you pretty confident? If you question yourself, why do you think that is? If you're pretty confident, why is that? Does it have to do more with your relationship with and knowledge of God, or with your own personality?

9. Is there someone in your life who criticizes your parenting skills? Does this person do so directly or indirectly? How do you handle it? Is there a better way to handle it?

Chapter 20—Abundance in the Home

1. What things are present in abundance in your home? Are you glad these things are so abundant?

2. Is your schedule overbooked? Do you feel stressed about it?

3. What takes up the most time in your schedule? Are these things you really want to be doing?

4. Have you checked with God to make sure these are things you really *need* to be doing? What might He be asking you to reduce or eliminate from your schedule?

5. Do you tend to try to accomplish things in your own strength? Why do you think this is?

6. Do you make sure you get alone time with God when you need it? Do you ask Him for His strength? Name a time where you've done this. Name a time when you didn't do this. How did the outcomes of the two situations differ?

7. Read the story of Peter walking on the water in Matthew 14:22-31. Do you identify with Peter? Why or why not?

8. Is your house as clean as you'd like it to be? If so, how has God made that possible? If not, are you trying your best?

9. How can God help you be content with the state of your home? Do you need Him to do this for you?

Chapter 21—Abundance in Relationships

1. Is your relationship with your husband abundant? What's abundant about it? What isn't abundant?

2. Read Ephesians 5:22-33. Does your marriage look like this? If not, what is your part in that?

3. Are there any ways in which you fail to honor your husband or simply don't treat him as if he's of first importance in your life? What are those ways?

4. Do you tend to provoke your children unnecessarily? Do you treat them as politely and respectfully as you would treat an adult stranger?

5. Do you know how each of your children best receives love? Do you proactively try to show them love in this way? If not, what could you do to start doing so?

6. Do you spend as much time with friends and family as you can? If not, why not?

7. When you're together with friends and family, what do you spend your time doing? Does it include encouraging one another?

8. Which relationships in your life are difficult (husband, children, family/friends)? What is difficult about them?

9. In what ways have your difficult relationships shown you that you need to be more like Christ? Are you willing to make these changes?

10. How have your difficult relationships positively affected your prayer life? Have you come to know God better through these relationships?

Acknowledgments

With Gratitude To:

My editor, Kim Bangs; Kristina Rees;
everyone who responded to my Facebook polls;
and those of you who read and critiqued chapters—you
all helped me at different times and with
different portions (sometimes difficult ones)
of this book. Thank you.

My husband, Phillip—for helping me carve out the time
to write, and for being the kind of husband who's part of
the abundance in my life. You're the greatest.

My children—you are part of that same abundance.
I love you so much.

About the Author

Megan Breedlove is the author of numerous devotionals and articles, both online and in print. With a heart for encouraging moms, Megan is a popular speaker at churches and women's groups. She graduated from Baylor University with a University Scholars degree (with an emphasis in psychology and foreign languages) and from Southwestern Baptist Theological Seminary with dual master's degrees in Marriage and Family Counseling and Religious Education. Megan and her husband, Phillip, reside in Fort Worth, Texas, with their five children, Ellie, 11; Kenny, 9; Lindsey, 8; Jessica, 6; and Timmy, 2. They attend Saint Andrew's Episcopal Church in Fort Worth. Megan enjoys reading, racquetball, cross-stitch, playing the piano, and studying foreign languages. To contact Megan, or to read her weekly uplifting devotionals, visit her website at www.MannaForMoms.com.

To contact the author, please visit the following:

Website: www.mannaformoms.com
Email: megan.breedlove@mannaformoms.com
Facebook: http://www.facebook.com/Megan.S.Breedlove
Twitter: http://twitter.com/MeganBreedlove

God, in His infinite mercy, has called me to encourage moms to glorify and enjoy Him in their daily lives. If your church or mother's group would like to receive that ministry through a personal visit, please contact me. I'd love to speak to your group in person.

I do not charge a "speaker's fee" as such. My husband and I believe that God's desire for us is to make His encouragement available to all, regardless of ability to pay. If a group is able to contribute toward my expenses, we ask them to do so. However, we don't want finances to prevent a group from requesting God's encouragement through me.

Also by
Megan Breedlove

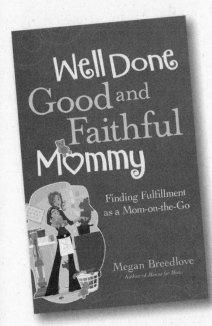

Well Done, Good and Faithful Mommy
Megan Breedlove
978.08307.66345

Before Megan became a mom, she knew parenting would be easy—and always rewarding. But when her first baby arrived, that bubble quickly burst. If you're like Megan, you've discovered that being a mom is tougher than it looks—and most of the time nobody notices what an incredible job you're doing! *Well Done, Good and Faithful Mommy* will show you how significant you really are—according to God, who always notices and never forgets to say so. You matter, Mommy … far more than you realize.

Manna for Moms
Megan Breedlove
978.08307.57633

Between diaper changes, carpools, meals and spills, you probably wonder if it's possible to find quality time with God. If only you could connect with your Creator and vacuum cereal out of the car seat at the same time. Megan Breedlove, a mom of five energetic little ones, has discovered the secret: Recognize He is there in every messy, miraculous moment. *Manna for Moms* is a devotional that will inspire you to look up and lighten up—even when you're cleaning up!

Available wherever books are sold!

Regal
God's Word for Your World™

Regal *for Women*

God's Word for a Woman's World

Hugs, Humor and Hope for Surviving Motherhood

mom
NEEDS
chocolate

Debora M. Coty

In mom-to-mom, smile-provoking style, humorist Debora M. Coty paints her offbeat picture of the realities of motherhood with a tangy twist, and offers outrageous coping tips, off-the-wall insights, sisterly hugs and warm encouragement. With witty frankness and wild abandon, she tackles a veritable grocery list of mud-between-your-toes issues. *Mom Needs Chocolate* will help you get back in touch with rejuvenating joy and empowering faith!

Mom Needs Chocolate • Debora M. Coty • 978.08307.45920

Your child's early years can be an exciting—and challenging—time for you as a parent. Fortunately, you don't have to do it on your own! God has a one-of-a-kind plan for the little life He has placed in your care, and it's never too soon to begin praying for this plan to unfold. *Praying Through Your Child's Early Years* will show you how.

Praying Through Your Child's Early Years
Jennifer Polimino and Carolyn Warren
978.08307.63894

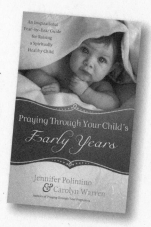

An Inspirational Year-by-Year Guide for Raising a Spiritually Healthy Child

Praying Through Your Child's Early Years

Jennifer Polimino & Carolyn Warren
Authors of Praying Through Your Pregnancy

THE COFFEE MOM'S DEVOTIONAL

A Rich Blend of Brief and Inspiring Devotions

CELESTE PALERMO

Each short, mommy-friendly reading in *The Coffee Mom's Devotional* is a reminder to drink in the fullness of God, allowing Him to sustain and enrich your life and fill it to overflowing. Whether you prefer coffee, diet soda, chai tea or Red Bull, there is something better—or rather, *Someone* better—to quench your thirst for abundant life. So grab a cup of your favorite beverage and get ready for a jolt of God's powerful, life-giving presence!

The Coffee Mom's Devotional • Celeste Palermo
978.08307.46460

Regal
God's Word for Your World™

Available wherever books are sold!